56-718

THE LIFE
OF
KATHLEEN
FERRIER

KATHLEEN FERRIER
A Portrait by Lotte Meitner-Graf

THE LIFE
OF
KATHLEEN
FERRIER

BY

HER SISTER

WINIFRED FERRIER

HAMISH HAMILTON
LONDON

94259

First published in Great Britain, 1955
by Hamish Hamilton Ltd.
90 Great Russell Street, London, W.C.1

Made and printed in Great Britain by Purnell & Sons Ltd.,
Paulton (Somerset) and London

CONTENTS

5

LIST OF ILLUSTRATIONS

ACKNOWLEDGMENTS

Thanks are due to Boosey and Hawkes Ltd. for kind permission to reproduce five bars from their edition of *The Rape of Lucretia* (music by Benjamin Britten, libretto by Ronald Duncan), to Novello & Co. Ltd., for permission to reproduce a passage from their edition of Handel's *Messiah* and to C. F. Kahnt Musikverlag, Bonn-am-Rhein, for permission to reproduce the opening bars of Mahler's song, *Um Mitternacht*.

PREFACE

IN October 1953, in order to establish a Memorial Fund, an appeal was made jointly by Sir John Barbirolli, Sir Laurence Olivier, Mr. Hamish Hamilton, Dame Myra Hess, Sir Benjamin Ormerod and Dr. Bruno Walter. In response came contributions from schools, women's institutes, choral societies, music clubs, gramophone societies and from thousands of individuals. Musicians from many countries offered their services for concerts. Dr. Bruno Walter flew from America to conduct jointly with Sir John Barbirolli a concert in the Royal Festival Hall. The directors of the Decca Record Company obtained permission from the B.B.C. and others, to make available for sale the recording of a broadcast on 5th June 1952. From these and many other efforts contributions were made to a Cancer Research Fund, associated with University College Hospital.

Many trophies were given for awards at Music Festivals throughout the country—some for piano playing, others for singing. There were about 1,000 entries for a prize in the form of musical training for a singer, offered by the *Daily Mail* and organised by the British Federation of Music Festivals.

The Post Office Music Society collected subscriptions from telephonists to provide three grand pianos in Fellowship of Remembrance Homes.

Under the administration of the Royal Philharmonic Society, a fund was opened to establish permanently a Memorial Scholarship for singers. To this fund Hamish Hamilton gave all the proceeds of the *Memoir,* edited by Neville Cardus, with contributions by Sir John Barbirolli, Benjamin Britten, Roy Henderson, Gerald Moore and Dr. Bruno Walter. Two annual scholarships were endowed in perpetuity, as a result.

All these things were done in tribute to Kathleen Ferrier.

Because of them, because of the widespread wish to know more about her both as a person and a singer and because of our close association throughout her life, this biography was written.

I have had generous help from relatives and many friends, only a few of whom could be mentioned in the text. To all of them I owe the deepest gratitude.

WINIFRED FERRIER

July 1955.

CHAPTER ONE

Kathleen Mary

IN 1845 Mary Ferrier, widow of Private Thomas Ferrier of the Royal Pembroke Militia Rifle Corps, fell down some steps in Tenby, South Wales. She died of her injuries, leaving three very young sons. Each was brought up by a local family; the second boy—also called Thomas—being taken under the wing of a clergyman. In due course Thomas was apprenticed to a tailor.

Having served his time he travelled the country, visiting one farm after another, making clothes for the farmers. Eventually he reached Micklehay farm near Blackburn. Some time later he married the farmer's daughter, Elizabeth Gorton, and they settled down to live in Blackburn.

At this time work on the railways seemed to have good prospects so Thomas forsook tailoring to become a guard on the trains running between Blackburn and Manchester. He was competent, reliable and hard-working: these qualities found expression in his job. He also had enterprising and ambitious ideas: these found outlet in the upbringing of his children. The two daughters were sent to work in the mill and the whole family made to live frugally, in order that the three sons could be sent to a teachers' training college in Chester. They went away to college with a great respect and longing for education, with austere religious views derived from their father and with their roots still firmly planted in the locality of their upbringing.

The second son, William, was an energetic, thickset man with a square jaw and curly dark red hair. He was friendly, sociable and had a sense of humour. He took pride in acquiring knowledge, had a good memory and never lost a child-like interest in the 'wonders of the world'. His college testimonials included a special reference to music:

I have much pleasure in testifying to the musical ability of Mr. William Ferrier: he has a good voice, an excellent ear and a ready knowledge of the theory of music.

Mr. Ferrier has given me much assistance by his singing in the chapel choir, and by rehearsing parts of the college chorus. In all his work I have found him earnest and thorough, and I have confidence that he will be highly successful in his teaching of music.

Theodore Ardern,
Music Master.

26th November 1890.   The College, Chester.

After completing his training in Chester, William returned to his home district, taking up his first post as a qualified assistant at St. Thomas's Church School, Blackburn.

In many a rural area in Britain during the nineteenth century it was said that folk could 'better themselves' by going to work in the towns. This idea reached the Murray family, who, in the middle of the century decided to move from Northern Ireland to Lancashire.

In those days, schooling for the majority was neither long nor effective. The Murray family sent their son James at the age of nine to work in a cotton mill. But this did not quench his lively spirit, his Irish ebullience. He grew up to be a tall, good-looking, ambitious man, with a sharp wit and a gift for telling a story. He enjoyed company and his love of fun made him a popular figure at parties and socials. He became an amateur pianist with a repertoire ranging from *Sweet Kiss Polka* to the music of Handel. He joined forces with a fiddler and a flautist, and the trio played for many local dances.

In his early twenties James Murray married Janet Knowles, a Scottish girl whose parents came from Ayrshire. The young couple were well matched, her native caution counteracting to some extent his impulsiveness. But when James was thirty-four years old, Janet died, leaving him with a daughter aged eight, and a son aged six. Their father was inconsolable: he lost interest in his home, dropped his music and spent most evenings at his club.

His daughter Alice took upon herself the task of looking after her younger brother Jim. One evening when they were playing in the kitchen before going to bed, Jim went too near to the fire and his night shirt caught alight. Alice threw him to the ground, rolled him in a rug and smothered the flames. Neither of them was seriously hurt, but Alice's hands were burnt. Though outwardly she appeared calm and reliable, this incident deepened the sense of insecurity caused by her mother's death.

Alice, a tall girl with grey eyes and shining black hair, was an inveterate organiser: Jim was to have an army career preferably in the 11th Hussars, like old Tom Rigby, a neighbour who was a survivor of 'The Charge'; and she herself would become a teacher. She practised on her younger brother and on as many of the neighbouring children as she could muster, and then at the age of fourteen left school, put up her hair and became a pupil teacher in St. Thomas' School. She began her work with the 'babies' class, helping with a hundred little boys and girls. They sat in long rows on raised galleries and she taught them to read, write and do sums on their slates.

In due course James Murray married again, his second wife having a prosperous dress-making business. They made their home over the shop but when three sons were born, Alice was called upon to help. Reluctantly she gave up teaching to become, in effect, foster mother to these three little boys. A cottage was found for her and her brothers in the little village of Wilpshire about three miles away.

The menage attracted some local interest. One day Alice, now about twenty, was pushing a pram with two babies in it and holding the hand of a toddler, when she was overtaken by an elderly woman. Putting a hand on the pram to help it up the hill and looking at Alice indignantly, she said: 'Your husband ought to be ashamed of himself. You're far too young to have three little children!'

Although tied to a home and family that were not her own,

and although thwarted in many of her natural desires, Alice loved the three boys dearly.

It was when she was about fourteen and whilst she was teaching that Alice Murray had first met William Ferrier. She had confided to her friend, Maud Lucas, that there was a rather nice man teaching in the boys' school. He was full of jokes, could sing well, and taught most of the music in the school. But he was quite old—nineteen or twenty!

The changes in her life did not prevent Alice seeing William. Somehow they managed to spend a good deal of time together. When the park lake was frozen they went skating and in summer there were picnics in the country around Wilpshire. They had many interests in common. William's musical activities spread to opera. He joined the local Operatic Society and began rehearsals for Iolanthe. Alice loved to act and to dance. She had a good contralto voice and would have liked to join the Operatic Society, but the three little boys could not be left alone.

Cheerfully William walked to Wilpshire and back two or three times a week. He had responsibilities to his widowed mother; Alice was tied to her home. In August 1900, however, after a courtship of nearly seven years, William Ferrier married Alice Murray.

Their parentage was such that they could claim for their children English, Welsh, Irish and Scottish blood. Although temperamentally they were very different, their marriage was happy; William was dutiful and conventional; Alice held unorthodox views on most subjects and was rebellious and aggressive. Her original turns of speech and mischievous ways amused her husband and he admired her independence and relied on her judgment. She was quick and impatient; he was calm and painstaking and did everything at a steady pace. 'He'll never have heart failure', she once said, 'but he'll make me have it!'

One Sunday soon after they were married, they were walking sedately home from church. 'I bet I can make you run,' said Alice. 'I bet you can't', William replied. Suddenly she ran to the nearest front door, knocked loudly and rushed up the street and round the corner. William had to run too, and found her leaning against a wall, helpless with laughter.

At this time William Ferrier was still an assistant teacher at St. Thomas's School, but his wife soon began to urge him to apply for a headship. Eventually he was appointed head of All Saints' School, Higher Walton, a small village on the old road between Blackburn and Preston.

The village owed its existence to a large cotton mill which stood at the bottom of a steep hill by the river. At the top of the hill was the church with the vicarage beside it. The owners of the mill had built two flat-fronted houses opposite the church: one for the mill-manager and the other for the schoolmaster. On each side of these houses stretched a straggly uneven line of cottages and small houses where the mill workers lived and at the corner was the village shop, 'Anna Maria's'.

The school stood in a side road and was built of local stone. It had thick walls and narrow Gothic windows. There was a large playground of beaten earth and cinders and beyond were fields and market gardens.

William Ferrier's life as a village schoolmaster suited him well. Although he had been brought up in the streets of a manufacturing town, he soon learned to identify every flower and bird to be seen for miles around Higher Walton. There was a real bond of affection between him and the sturdy, well-cared-for school children, with whom he spent many happy hours wandering around the fields and lanes.

Most of the parents were employed in the cotton mill and were hard-working, God-fearing people, for whom William Ferrier had a great liking and respect. So many of his ex-pupils corresponded with him for long periods after they had left school that 'Our father's old boys' or 'old girls' became one of the family jokes.

The school was small and so was the salary—so small, in fact, that William Ferrier, in order to supplement it, had to teach on four nights a week at evening school. He also instructed the men's class on Sunday, sang in the choir and acted as church-warden. It was a very busy life but he somehow managed to cope with it all without giving the impression of being hurried or overworked.

The village was three miles from the nearest town—Preston.

A local 'character', Whalley, ran a bus there once or twice a week, but its times were erratic. Whalley's bus was a two-horse waggonette with the entrance at the rear up two rather high steps. The passengers sat eight on each side facing one another and there was room for another three outside with the driver. As the bus bumped and jolted its way home from Preston, a passenger would often begin to sing. The others with their natural feeling for harmony would join in, and the people who lived in the isolated farms and cottages along the way would hear strains of *Drink to me Only* or *Sweet and Low*, sung by folks who loved music and could sing well.

Alice Ferrier settled down happily enough in the school-house. Her first child, a boy, was still-born and this was a terrible disappointment and grief to her. When later a daughter, Winifred, was born she was delighted and yet so over-anxious that she used to waken the baby to reassure herself that it was alive. When Winifred was two-and-a-half years old, another child was born, named George.

One day notice came from the mill-owners that the rent of the school-house was to be raised from 5s. 9d. a week to 6s. 3d.—a serious matter for a man earning only £120 a year, and with a wife and two small children to keep. William took it for granted that he would have to pay it, but his wife was indignant. The house was large with stone floors and long passages. It was difficult to heat, to keep clean, and the noise of the church bells echoed through it, waking up the children and setting her nerves jangling. Didn't her husband work all hours of the day and night —because the salary was so small—and act as an unpaid curate? He deserved not an increase in rent but a house rent-free!

With energy and determination she searched around and eventually found a smaller, cheaper and more convenient house, nearly two miles outside the village. William uncomplainingly walked or cycled to and from school, and later on, Win sat happily on the carrier behind him while George pedalled along on a tricycle by his side.

By the time she had reached her fortieth year Mrs. Ferrier had concluded that she was to have no more children. But she was disappointed to have only two. No sooner, however, had she given her cot away to a village woman who had had twins, than she found to her joy that she *was* to have another child. Realising in these circumstances the inconvenience of being two miles outside the village, she set about finding yet another house, this time just on the outskirts. The family moved into No. 1 Bank Terrace, Higher Walton, Lancashire.

It was there that, during the morning of the 22nd April, 1912, Alice Ferrier had her second daughter. On Whit Sunday—after much discussion about names—she was christened Kathleen Mary.

CHAPTER TWO

Fourteen

KATHLEEN FERRIER was a healthy baby with grey-blue eyes, flaxen hair and a high forehead. As a toddler, alert and full of energy, she showed a lively personality, needing no encouragement to 'do a party piece'. When her grandmother came visiting, Kathleen seemed to feel it her job to entertain, often standing on the sofa to sing and recite for her. The role of entertainer—the family being the first audience—was to persist throughout her life.

Her mother could also be gay and witty, but after ten years in a small village where there were few congenial people and no music except occasional amateur concerts, she felt that she had vegetated long enough. By the time Kathleen was eighteen months old, Mrs. Ferrier showed the signs of restlessness which presaged a complete change.

Her restlessness was increased by a number of factors affecting the family life. She was concerned about her children's education. The nearest secondary school was in Preston and could only be reached by a long bus or cycle ride. There was no teacher of pianoforte or dancing in the village and, like many parents, she was determined that her children should have all the opportunities that her own childhood had lacked. She persuaded her husband to apply for the headship of St. Paul's School, Blackburn. He was appointed, and early in 1914 the family moved.

Although for a short time the two older children missed the freedom of the country life that they had known, they soon settled down to their new surroundings. Mrs. Ferrier was satisfied: there was a good High School for girls, a Grammar School for boys and plenty of social life.

Kathleen pattered happily round the house, talking, singing and asking questions. She was cherished both by her parents and by her sister and brother, but she soon became conscious that there were many things that she must learn in order to catch up with them.

When she was about three years old she began to play the piano. She would dance up to the instrument, play a few notes and then dance round the room and this she would repeat over and over again. One day when her cousin Trixie came to call, Kathleen said to her, 'Shall I play for you, Trixie?' She sat down and picked out a tune with one finger, then suddenly burst into a passion of tears. Trix comforted her and said, 'What's the matter, love?' 'I want to play,' said Kathleen, 'and I can't play *properly*!'

When her sister had a craze for swimming, Kathleen wanted to learn too. She was about four years old when Win took her to the baths for the first time. Win, who was tall for her eleven years, jumped into four feet of water, intending to lift her little sister in. She turned round to see a small surprised face just disappearing under water. Even at that early age, Kathleen tended to assume that she could accomplish anything she wished to do.

About this time homework began to loom large in the family life. Win settled down for a couple of hours every evening at her books. George, when closely questioned, admitted reluctantly that he had 'a bit of Latin' to do. Kathleen felt that it was her job to learn to read. She followed her mother round the house, book in hand, pointing to a word and saying, 'What does this one say?', and the result was that, before she was old enough to go to school she could read quite well.

When she was five Kathleen was sent to St. Silas' Elementary School, Blackburn. After a few months, however, her mother heard a rumour that the school was unhealthy. She was always nervous about her children's health, particularly Kathleen's. This rumour was enough to cause a transfer to 'Crosshill', the kindergarten department of the Girls' High School. Paying fees for this school meant a real sacrifice: in the wartime conditions of 1917, Mrs. Ferrier, in addition to helping her husband to run a play centre in the evenings, took a job at the Recruiting Centre.

In spite of the extra that she earned, money was a major pre-occupation; food and clothing were very expensive. Winifred was at the High School and although she held a bursary, it did not pay for all the books, clothes and shoes that she needed. George had entered the Grammar School and was growing so fast that it cost as much to feed and clothe him as if he were a man.

Kathleen too was big for her age and often preferred to play with boys, but she had a friend, Mary Chadwick, who lived across the road. When Mary organised a sale in her backyard, for Dr. Barnardo's Homes, Kathleen took charge of the gate money—a halfpenny entrance fee—and kept off and eventually chased away some boys who were trying to gatecrash.

Many happy evenings were spent in Mary's house, drawing, painting, playing at 'schools', and sometimes reading stories to Mary and her little sister Joan. Like most children Kathleen had crazes for one thing after another—skipping-ropes, whips and tops, hoops and hop-scotch.

One day Kathleen came home from school in great trepidation. She had borrowed a scooter and after riding it for some time, wearing out the sole of her right shoe in the process, she had crouched down and leant against the back wheel. The further result was a large hole in the back of her gym slip.

Her mother was furious. Gym slips were expensive, so she had taken the trouble to make this one out of a remnant of serge. There was no material left to put in a new back or even to patch the hole. To make a new slip would need time and money and she was short of both.

Margaret, Kathleen's cousin, who had come home with her to provide moral support, added fuel to the flames by saying, 'Kath couldn't help it'. She was promptly sent packing. This incident taught Kathleen a lesson she never forgot—that clothes cost money and money is hard to earn and must never be spent recklessly. But in spite of all the worry and strain of bringing up children in these circumstances, there was plenty of fun and no lack of affection in the family.

Kathleen grew into a tall sturdy girl with straight fair hair and a wide infectious smile. Her irrepressible sense of humour sometimes got her into trouble at school and when she came home, she would be bubbling over with news. 'Mother,' she would begin, as soon as she reached the front door, 'what d'you think happened today?' and she would proceed to tell some funny incident, mimicking the people involved.

One day, however, it was a story of a different kind. 'Mother,' she began as usual from the front door, 'you know you always say "Speak the truth and shame the devil". Well, I did, and I'm in trouble!'

Apparently one of the teachers who was given to strong personal likes and dislikes had reduced one of Kathleen's friends to tears by crossing out all her sums and giving her no marks out of ten. Seeing her friend's distress, Kathleen, scarlet with rage, leapt to her feet, saying loudly, 'This is more than flesh and blood can stand. Amy has exactly the same answers as I have and you've given me ten out of ten and Amy none. I just can't stand it!'

The resulting scene can be imagined.

Before she started to attend school, Kathleen had begun to pick out tunes by ear, using the thumb and two fingers of her right hand and moving up and down the piano with great speed and nimbleness. A friend of the family, who thought she deserved to be encouraged, bought her 'Smallwood's Piano Tutor' and taught her the names of the notes. From this book Kathleen learnt to read music and play some simple tunes. Mrs. Ferrier became convinced that her daughter was unusually gifted, and decided that she must have the best possible teacher.

At that time Miss Frances Walker was famous in the North of England for the success of her pupils both in examinations and at Musical Festivals. Mrs. Ferrier went to see her, taking Kathleen, now aged nine. When she was asked if Kathleen could have lessons, Miss Walker replied that she did not take beginners. But Mrs. Ferrier persisted and in the end Miss Walker, having been much amused by Kathleen's unconventional fingering, agreed to accept her as a pupil. Nothing could have proved more fortunate.

Kathleen soon began to go over to Mary Chadwick's house to play. Mary's Uncle John was a piano enthusiast, who, when

Paderewski came to England, used to follow him from one concert to another. He was delighted with Kathleen's playing and when she had finished he always shook her solemnly by the hand. Years later Kathleen told Mary that when he did so, he always slipped a shilling into her hand with a wink to her to say nothing about it.

When a school choir was formed, all the girls were tested individually. The music mistress heard Kathleen sing and said, 'Yes, I will have you in the choir, because you keep in tune—but be careful to sing softly. Your voice is husky.'

Kathleen led a very full, interesting and happy school life, enjoying literature and taking easily to French, Latin and mathematics. She learnt quickly and because of this was often in 'trouble'. Having finished her work she was never short of ways of amusing herself—and her classmates. She played in the Junior Netball Team, sang in the school choir and found time to join the Girl Guides. Years later she would talk with relish of the meals that she and her friends used to cook over the camp fire.

She was fascinated by facial contortions. In those days many of the women who worked amid the great noise of the weaving sheds developed lip reading, which enabled them to hold long conversations in dumb show. Sometimes two of them sitting one at each end of the tramcar could be seen 'talking' with lively, animated gestures and without uttering a sound. Kathleen would watch, completely absorbed, and would then go home and imitate them, adding exaggerated and amusing details of her own.

She developed much mobility of expression and control over the muscles of her face. When later she was at the telephone switchboard, where talking was forbidden, she found it quite useful to be able to 'talk' to the next girl without making a sound. It is probable too, that this long practice helped her, when she was singing, to make her words clearly heard. Kathleen took the keenest delight in playing with words: she collected limericks and 'funny' stories.

All this time she was making steady progress with her piano lessons. She was successful in a number of examinations and began to compete as a pianist at local Musical Festivals. In

Lancashire at that time there was an unusually large number of
very good pianists of about Kathleen's age. They met regularly
at festivals: there was great rivalry between them. Kathleen was
usually somewhere among the top four.

Mr. and Mrs. Ferrier had denied themselves all their lives in
order to pay school and music fees for their children. Kathleen's
piano lessons were expensive and must continue whatever
happened. But, if she stayed at school and college until she was
twenty, as Win had done, her father would be sixty-five by the
time she was trained. Mrs. Ferrier wanted him to be able to
retire before then.

And so the decision was taken that Kathleen should leave
school at fourteen and enter the Post Office as a probationer.
Mrs. Ferrier chose this job, not because she thought it would be
interesting, but because it was a safe job with a pension. She had
a deep rooted feeling of insecurity.

The staff at the High School were much concerned at this
decision. It seemed a waste that a girl with such ability should
not be able to go to a university. Kathleen's form mistress pointed
out to her that she was capable of excelling in any subject that
she chose if she remained at school. She warned her that she might
find telephone work dull. Kathleen listened but said nothing.

Mrs. Ferrier, when interviewed by the headmistress, was
adamant and did not reveal the other reason for her decision.
Her son George had always caused the family anxiety. He had
done badly at school and had shown no desire to train for any
profession. His only wish was to see the world and, after he had
run away from home three times, he had been sent to Canada
under an Emigration Farming scheme. His parents worried
constantly about him, though they told no one, and they expected
at any time to have to send him passage money home. They also
realised that if he came home, he would need some sort of
training too. This, more than anything else, made them feel
that another six years of expense for Kathleen was more than
they could face.

Kathleen accepted the decision with a typical lack of resentment. In July 1926—when she was fourteen—her schooldays
ended.

CHAPTER THREE

Twenty-three

LEAVING school involves a bigger change than starting school. The second stage in life means forsaking the world of children for that of adults. For a time Kathleen was miserable at the Post Office in Blackburn. She missed her friends and the interesting and varied life that her school had provided.

As a girl probationer in the telegraph room, her duties included distributing telegrams, addressing envelopes and collecting dockets from the telephonists. Gradually, she adapted herself and became happier. Sometimes, as she made her way along the line of girls sitting with their faces to the switchboard, she would whisper out of the corner of her mouth, 'Have you heard this one?' She became popular with the girls but not always so with the supervisor.

The telegrams were typed on the second floor; it was her job to fold them, put them in an envelope and send them by chute to the ground floor. She boasted that if she made a mistake, she could run down the stone stairs two at a time and catch the telegram before it went out.

At the time she said nothing about her job which would worry or upset her parents. Rather did she remember the amusing incidents and stories that circulated in the Post Office, telling them at home with gusto, to her father's especial delight.

Mrs. Ferrier had no patience with spoiled and undisciplined children; though she was passionately devoted to her own, she never gave in to their little failings. If they were slightly off colour, she would say, 'Work it off!' But when there was something seriously wrong, she was so distressed that they did their best to hide it, so as to avoid a fuss. At fourteen, Kathleen had acquired a habit of self control and reserve which helped her to deal with the problem of her daily work—the first big trial of her life.

In her early teens there came some awareness of the conflicting characteristics within her. One might well ask if these were inherited from her Irish, Scottish, Welsh and Lancashire ancestry. Her mind once made up, however, then nothing would shake her determination. Quietly and firmly she would persist, without aggression or resentment, until she got her own way.

She managed to find time for some energetic outdoor activities. As well as being an enthusiastic member of the Girl Guides, she enjoyed swimming and played tennis well enough to be included in the Post Office Club team. Match play suited her: she usually did better as a result of 'nerves'.

The members of her family found their own amusements at home and when visits were made to their cousins, the three daughters of Maud and George Ferrier, who lived about a mile away, there was no lack of entertainment. Trix and Dorothy had good soprano voices, Margaret was interested in elocution, Kathleen played the piano and Win the violin. When they had all performed individually, they would gather round the piano and sing through the well-known songs of the Gilbert and Sullivan operas. *Iolanthe* was a favourite, and William and George who still remembered their parts in the opera would join in the chorus.

Kathleen played the accompaniments for these choruses and joined in the singing. At this time her voice was strong but still rather husky. 'I believe our Kath's going to have a contralto voice', her mother said on one occasion, 'and I love a contralto'.

Music was now Kathleen's main interest. Her liking for competition drew her to the festivals. These provided valuable opportunities for getting used to performing in public. Any harm that might have been done by their competitive nature was counteracted by Miss Walker's concern for her wider musical culture and her insistence that success at festivals was only a means to an end—a wider and deeper and more sensitive interpretation of music.

While she was still only fourteen years of age she passed the final grade of the Associated Board of the Royal Academy of

Music and the Royal College of Music—'an unprecedented success for so youthful a student' as a press notice put it.

When she was sixteen, the *Daily Express* organised a national competition for piano playing. Kathleen entered along with many of her contemporaries who regularly competed at the local musical festivals. The north regional contest took place in Manchester and the competition was exceptionally close. Two of the competitors had to be recalled and asked to repeat their performances.

The *Blackburn Times* of 1st December 1928, reporting the competition said

A YOUNG BLACKBURN MUSICIAN

Those who have the gift of dreaming dreams and seeing visions of Blackburn's musical future must be greatly comforted by some significant signs of her musical present. We have many young people in the town today giving evidence of real musical ability, and every now and then something demonstrates that we have a few who possess outstanding gifts in one or other department of the realm which is world wide.

Today I have heard that Miss Kathleen Ferrier, daughter of Mr. W. Ferrier, headmaster of St. Paul's school, and pupil of Miss F. E. Walker, the well known teacher of pianoforte, has won a piano in a national competition for piano playing. There were 20,000 entries in the competition organised by the *Daily Express*, and Miss Ferrier, who is only 16 years of age, has won her prize in Grade B of it. I offer my heartiest congratulations to Miss Ferrier and her very gifted music mistress on the distinction she has attained.

The winners in each area were awarded an upright piano made by a famous British maker. There was then a final competition in London to decide which of the 72 winners should have the six grand pianos offered. Accommodation and travelling expenses to London for the competitor and a parent were provided and arrangements made for the contest to take place in the Wigmore Hall.

When the time for the London contest came, Mrs. Ferrier was ill. Win, who took her mother's place, was somewhat worried by the responsibility of being in charge of the party on so important an occasion, and sewed her money into a pocket in her underclothes.

This was Kathleen's first visit to London: she never forgot it.

On arrival at Euston, the sisters took a taxi to the Russell Hotel, which so impressed them by its magnificence that they began to wonder whether they had arrived at the wrong place. Perhaps there was another, more modest, Russell Hotel? But as they stood doubtfully in the entrance, they heard to their great relief that someone was playing one of the competition test pieces.

The next morning the competitors gathered at the Wigmore Hall, among them Cyril Smith and Phyllis Sellick, who were destined to make great names for themselves as pianists. Kathleen was nervous. She walked across the platform to the piano, a tall figure with straight, fair hair and a face almost green with nervous tension, her long jaw-line set in determination. She played well but was not on top of her form, and when the six winners were announced her name was not among them.

To cheer themselves up after this disappointment, Kathleen and Win went to see a performance of *Show Boat* at the Drury Lane Theatre. As soon as Paul Robeson began to sing, Kathleen's eyes filled with tears and having begun to cry she found it impossible to stop. The relief from nervous tension and the sadness of his voice were too much for her. In the bus on the way back to the hotel she recovered sufficiently to say between sobs, 'Wasn't he pathetic!' And when they reached the hotel there was a telegram from Miss Walker which read: 'Never mind, love, you've done your best'. This re-started the flow of tears.

Kathleen was easily moved by beauty and sadness. She found it almost unbearable to be deeply stirred and avoided going to plays and films if she knew that they were sad. 'I'm not going if it's "heart-rendering"', she used to say.

The piano which she had won, a Cramer, was exhibited for some time in the window of a music shop in Blackburn. When at last it was delivered to her home, the well-worn family one was relegated to a spare room and a party was held to celebrate and to christen the new one. At this party were two friends who were to play a decisive role in Kathleen's life. Annie Chadwick was a fine soprano singer who had been trained in Italy. Her husband, Tom Barker, had a rich and powerful baritone voice. They were both good musicians and were in great demand in East Lancashire for concerts and for oratorio.

They had much in common with Kathleen: love of a game of cards, sense of humour and a passion for music. Kathleen spent many evenings with them, and became an enthusiastic and competent accompanist. The more florid and complicated the accompaniments were, the more she enjoyed mastering them.

At that time Tom and Annie gave many concerts in Sunday schools and under the auspices of the Co-operative Educational Society. They joined forces with a tenor and a contralto and gave solos, duets, trios and quartets. Kathleen practised the accompaniments very thoroughly and was engaged, on one never-to-be-forgotten evening, as accompanist for a concert in Burnley.

The tenor, who had not heard her play, was somewhat worried when he saw the new eighteen-year-old accompanist, but all went well, and after the concert there was general satisfaction. Kathleen was intoxicated by it all and from then on she became a regular member of the party. Sometimes she played piano solos and, she even sang the fifth part in the quintet *Love is meant to make us glad* when it was included in the programme.

Kathleen enjoyed every minute of the concerts. She liked the journeys and the excitement of changing and preparing. She thrived on the companionship of people with a like passion for music and a sense of humour as broad as her own. With the appetite of a young girl who often rushed straight from work to the platform without a meal, she revelled in the lavish Lancashire suppers which were usually served in the interval. There was one red-letter-day, when the artists were given two suppers!

Two months after her eighteenth birthday the following letter arrived:

June 1930

I have to inform you that you have been appointed telephonist on probation as from the 8th June 1930 on scale 15.0d to 35.0d.

Your commencing pay will be 19.0d. a week and your date of increment the 22nd April.

C. Harvey. Head Postmaster.

After this she took her place at the switchboard and when she became known to the regular subscribers, there were several men who would ring her up for the pleasure of hearing her voice. Sometimes she had to change duties with other telephonists or pay them to take her place, so that she could continue her musical activities. In addition to singing in the choir and acting as accompanist, she continued her piano lessons, taking the A.R.C.M. and L.R.A.M. diplomas in 1929 and 1931, playing at local celebrity concerts and entering for festivals.

She played Brahms's *Scherzo in E flat Minor* at Liverpool Festival in May 1930 and won the Gold Medal. At Lytham the following month she won the first prize. John Wills, the adjudicator, said: 'The tone was fluent and the general effect very musical.'

On 3rd July 1930 she broadcast for the first time, taking part in a concert in the Manchester studios as a pianist. Her programme included Brahms's *Scherzo in E flat Minor* and Percy Grainger's *Shepherd's Hey*.

One evening when she went to rehearse she said to Annie Chadwick, 'Will you teach me to sing?' Annie was surprised and laughed, but Kathleen was serious, and was given some lessons. She began with the rudiments of singing technique, but at that time her voice had no outstanding quality.

She also joined the James Street Congregational Church Choir to which Tom and Annie belonged. The choirmaster at that time was Mr. Albert Higham, a music lover and a friend of Sir Hamilton Harty. Kathleen sang in the choir in many performances of oratorio and in 1931, in a performance of *Elijah* conducted by Harold Marsden, was chosen to sing in the trio *Lift Thine Eyes*. 'Imagine me singing this', she said, 'I shall never be a singer!' Before their entry, the girl sitting next to Kathleen whispered, 'Are your knees knocking?' 'Knocking', said Kathleen, 'they're playing *God Save the King*!'

The report of the event in the local paper read: 'Miss Ferrier sang pleasingly in the trio *Lift Thine Eyes* and more will be heard in Blackburn of this young vocalist.'

All this time Kathleen began to respond to music with increasing intensity. The first hearing of music which appealed to her was a revelation in which she was absorbed and lost. When it ended she seemed to return with difficulty to a realisation of her surroundings.

Sometimes she conveyed this intensity of insight and emotion to those who were listening to her piano playing. On one occasion she played the *Moonlight Sonata* at a concert arranged by Miss Walker. At the end, when she took her hands from the keys, there was a moment of silence before the applause, some of those present feeling that in her was a power, a spirit rich in its capacity to communicate, to interpret life itself through music.

When Kathleen was twenty a Celebrity Concert was held in King George's Hall, Blackburn. She enjoyed playing for Elsie Ackland the contralto and Harold Noble the baritone. But the highlight of the evening for her was playing with Louis Godowsky, the famous violinist. She found it most exciting to partner so fine a musician. The *Blackburn Times* reported: 'As accompanist of all three artists Kathleen Ferrier enhanced a reputation which in her early teens stood very high.'

About this time she took the part of King Arthur in three performances of a Girl Guides' play in the Blackburn Lecture Hall. Half way through the final performance one of the curtains, which had been pushed against a spotlight, began to smoulder. Suddenly it burst into flames which swept to the roof and round one side of the stage. A few children screamed and made a rush for the door. Without hesitation Kathleen walked to the front of the stage and called to the audience to remain calm. Some of the Girl Guides ran to the hydrants in the corridor and turned them on, and in no time the fire was extinguished. Having turned on the water the Guides were unable to turn it off again and by the time the fire brigade arrived the front of the hall was ankle deep in water. The members of the company, still in their costumes and grease paint, splashed their way out of the hall. 'Well,' said Kathleen, 'thank goodness it happened at the *last* performance and not at the *first*!'

It was a great blow when Annie and Tom Barker left Blackburn and moved to Wolverhampton, but at the beginning of 1934 Kathleen herself was transferred to the Post Office at Blackpool, twenty-seven miles away. She moved into 'digs' and, so that she could reach home easily, bought a bicycle, paying half a crown a week out of her small wage until it was paid for.

At that time table tennis had become something more than a parlour game and some of the telephonists became interested

KATHLEEN, AGED
ONE, WITH HER MOTHER,
SISTER WINIFRED AND
BROTHER GEORGE

HER PARENTS' WEDDING GROUP

AT CROSSHILL, 1921
Kathleen in left foreground

THE CHOIR, BLACKBURN HIGH SCHOOL
Kathleen centre of back row

AGED 17

AS KING ARTHUR IN A GIRL GUIDES' PLAY

AGED 19

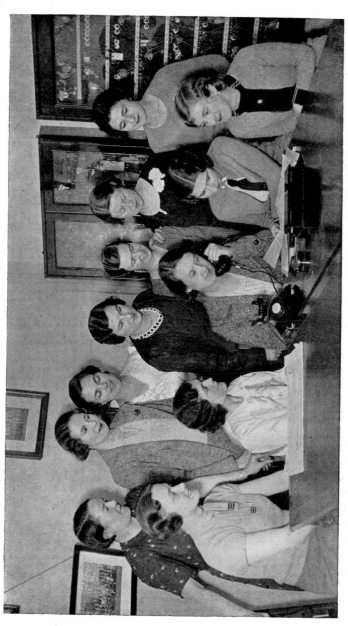

THE BLACKPOOL ENTRANTS FOR THE 'TIM' CONTEST, 1934

Kathleen seated on left

WITH HER FATHER AND MOTHER

'OUR FATHER'
Taken by Kathleen

CYCLING HOME

GOLF AT HASTE HILL

WORKINGTON FESTIVAL, 1938

ON HOLIDAY, 1938

and took private lessons. The Post Office eventually produced a good team and with Kathleen as captain joined the Blackpool league, playing in many matches. She also played lawn tennis for the office team.

In 1935 Kathleen was one of three telephonists chosen from the North-West area to demonstrate the use of telephones at a Post Office Exhibition which lasted for a month. This was one of the happiest times in her Post Office career. At about the same time the Golden Voice competition was held to find a suitable voice for the speaking clock, TIM. Of the twelve entrants from the Blackpool office, one was chosen for the final. But it was not Kathleen: in the excitement of the moment, she said afterwards, she had put in an extra aspirate in the reading test.

Although continuing to play the piano and act as an accompanist, she became more and more impelled by a desire to sing. In 1935 she decided to enter for Blackpool Festival in the Tudor Class. In this competition the singers were required to play their own accompaniments. In preparation, Kathleen took singing lessons with Mr. Thomas L. Duerden, who had married her cousin Margaret. He was organist and choir master at St. John's Church where her uncle sang in the choir, and he also conducted very good boys' and men's choirs.

She had high hopes of doing well at this contest. Playing the accompaniment required so little effort on her part that she felt able to concentrate all her attention on the singing. But when the contest was held before Sir Richard Terry she was not successful. No comments were made on her voice.

This was a terrible setback. She knew that her playing was good. At twenty-three her voice must be mature. It looked as though her desire to sing was doomed to disappointment. She said little at the time, and in later years never mentioned this episode. Her disappointment bit deeply.

Along what way did her future now lie? At the telephone switchboard she made bets with herself on how quickly she could put subscribers through. But after nine years she had found no prospects which satisfied her.

*   *   *

B

At one of her concerts Kathleen had met a young man who lived a few miles from Blackburn and had become friendly with him and his family. When it became obvious that she was contemplating marriage with him, those who knew her best tried to dissuade her. They felt that she was young and unsophisticated for her age and that she had not met enough men to be able to choose wisely; also that, as he was not a musician, he was not the right man for her. Nevertheless on 19th November 1935, at the age of twenty-three, she married.

CHAPTER FOUR

Two Octaves

THE newly-married Wilsons moved into a little house in Warton. Kathleen appeared to settle down happily to domesticity. Dusting and polishing gave her satisfaction and she enjoyed cooking. For the first time she had a garden and set out with great enthusiasm to cultivate it. She read a good deal about the subject, and gradually the garden began to take shape. The diminutive lawn which she grew from seed was a particular source of pride.

Kathleen and her husband joined the Lytham Vocal Society, cycling every Tuesday evening from Warton for the rehearsal of Elgar's *King Olaf* and having supper and a musical evening with friends afterwards. On being asked to sing at a Mothers Union social, she said, 'I only sing in the chorus. I'm not a soloist.' Eventually however she was persuaded to sing *Bless this House.*

Soon Kathleen's husband was transferred to a bank in Silloth, twenty-three miles from Carlisle. Kathleen was now without a garden, but she enjoyed living in Silloth. Although a small town it had a life and character of its own and she made many good friends.

She joined the Dramatic Society. Once, when they were short of men, she took the part of a remover's man. Dressed in a coat and trousers and with her hair hidden under a cap, she walked on, rolled and picked up a carpet and walked out with it. That was the extent of the part. On another occasion when they played *The Deaf Man,* she took the part of the scolding wife whose pie is eaten, and also made the pie!

Silloth has some fine golf links lying along the shore of the

Solway Firth. With her usual energy and enthusiasm Kathleen began to learn to play. Soon she was entering for tournaments and winning prizes. She revelled in these matches and her golf improved rapidly.

At the tennis club about this time, she met Jack and Wyn Hetherington, who became her close friends. One day a picnic was arranged with them and their little son, Peter, then about three years old. They were nearly ready to start when Jack found that a button was missing from his coat. Wyn was busy putting the final touches to the lunch so Kathleen offered to sew on the button. Peter leaned against her knee watching the needle fly in and out. As with a final twist she wound the cotton round the button and fastened it off, he looked up at her and said, with respect and surprise in his voice, 'Klever Kaff!' This so amused Kathleen that she adopted the title ever afterwards, often signing herself K.K. The alliteration delighted her.

Win, who spent many holidays at Silloth, wondered sometimes if Kathleen was happy. She was as lively and humorous as usual, but when her face was in repose, which was seldom, there seemed to be a new expression of sadness. Was it perhaps because she, who loved children, had so far had none? Win knew her better than to ask questions, being sure that they would be brushed away with a joke.

When it became known that Kathleen was a pianist, the choral society asked her to play their accompaniments. This she did both on the piano and the organ. She began to teach a few children to play the piano but, although she was fond of them, she found teaching wearisome. It was difficult for her to under-stand and sympathise with those who could only learn slowly. When one of these slow ones was stumbling through a piece, she would walk to the window to try to catch the eye of her friend Eleanor Coyd, who kept a dress shop over the way. She would convey her feelings by pointing over her shoulder to the struggling pianist, and making comical gestures of agony and despair.

Kathleen soon had a circle of friends who came often to spend musical evenings in the flat over the bank. Sometimes she would amuse them by changing key every few bars when she was playing their accompaniments. Then, with exaggerated, florid arpeggios, with scoops and trills, she would do her imitation of a screaming soprano. The next moment she would be playing Beethoven or Bach with complete absorption.

She began to practise the piano seriously once more and in the belief that a definite objective would help her to keep up her standard, decided to enter for the Carlisle Festival. When her husband bet her a shilling that she dare not enter for the singing contest, she accepted his challenge and put her name down for the contralto solo class.

In March 1937 she won in both entries: the Dr. Lediard Memorial Trophy in the pianoforte section for her playing of Thiman's *Sarabande* and Arensky's *Study in F sharp*; and the Silver Rose Bowl, presented by Lady Mabel Howard, for the best singer of the Festival. Mr. Maurice Jacobson who judged the piano class and who, with Mr. Yeaman Dodds, awarded the Rose Bowl, told Kathleen that she had a very beautiful voice, one of the finest he had heard, and that she ought to make singing her career. Thus it came about that during March 1937 her life reached a turning point.

After her success at Carlisle she was offered engagements to sing locally, taking part in performances of *Messiah* and *Elijah*. At a Harvest Festival, for singing *Thank God for a Garden*, she received her first fee—one guinea.

One day she ran across the road to her friends Eleanor and Bill Coyd and said: 'Here's a letter asking me to sing and wanting to know what my fee is. What shall I say?' 'I should put your fee up,' said Bill, 'you've got travelling expenses and music and dresses to buy. I should say three guineas.' 'Right, I'll do that,' said Kathleen, 'and I'll make you my business manager.'

A few days later she again dashed across the road and waving the reply said, 'Bill, you're sacked! They say they can't pay three guineas! They've turned me down.'

Kathleen continued to compete at festivals and Wyn Hetherington often drove her to them. On one occasion in Blackpool, Kathleen felt uncertain about her song, so they searched for a studio, and when she had rehearsed felt better. But after the contest she came back to Wyn and said, 'I know I haven't done well. My breathing was poor. The girl who sang fifth will win. She sang beautifully.' This judgment proved right; Kathleen came second.

In 1938, at the Workington Festival, she sang *Silent Noon* by Vaughan Williams and won the Gold Cup. A month later, at the Millom Festival, she was awarded the Gold Medal for her singing of *Secrecy* by Hugo Wolf. Maurice d'Oisley who adjudicated said, 'This is a beautiful voice, full of colour and lovely warm velvety quality. The melodic rendering was excellent and the phrasing almost perfect. Her words were clear and charged with meaning. Her voice is lovely. It makes me imagine I am being stroked.'

In December 1938, in Workington Opera House, she took part in a charity concert, entitled *Artists you might never have heard*. It was attended by Cecil McGivern, then B.B.C. producer at Newcastle, who was looking for local talent, and also by W. S. Newall, a Whitehaven reporter, who had already compered two radio shows featuring Cumberland life.

Later Mr. McGivern told Win of that occasion. He had been sitting for nearly three-and-a-half hours listening to a succession of pianists, comedians, guitar and accordion players, violinists and choirs. Then the curtains swung apart again and a girl in a white dress stood there quite still. When she began to sing *Curly Headed Babby,* the effect on him was electrifying. She was, he realised at once, outstanding both in voice and personality. He lost no time in arranging for her to broadcast in the near future.

Sitting behind Mr. McGivern at this concert were Kathleen's parents; her father smiling and confident, her mother tense with anxiety. They were delighted to hear Mr. McGivern's opinion of their daughter's performance and looked forward to hearing her first broadcast. But before it took place Mrs. Ferrier became very ill, and at the beginning of February 1939 she died.

Mr. Ferrier, who was by this time seventy-one, went to live in London with Win, but her flat was small and he was alone all day, so Kathleen suggested that he should go to live with her and her husband in Silloth. This arrangement worked well and he enjoyed life there very much. He was most interested in what went on in the docks, watched for hours while the cargoes were loaded and discharged and talked to anyone who had time to spare. In a very short while he learnt much about the history and geography of Silloth and the surrounding countryside. He took a great interest and pride in Kathleen's musical activities, spending much time in copying out and transposing songs for her.

Kathleen's first broadcast as a singer took place on the 23rd February 1939, when she sang *Curly Headed Babby*, *Mighty Like a Rose* and with the Millom Male Voice Choir *The End of a Perfect Day*. For this broadcast the performers were collected in two motor coaches and taken to the Newcastle studio. When it was over the artists boarded the coaches for home. Kathleen who lived at the end of the route arrived back at 4 a.m. After this she persuaded her father to buy a small car, which facilitated further journeys to Newcastle, where she sang in seven more programmes, taking part in shows called *Quick Change* and *All the Best*.

In April 1939 Kathleen again entered for the Carlisle Festival. The test piece was *All Souls' Day* by Richard Strauss. Dr. Hutchinson, speaking for himself and his co-adjudicator, Dr. Armstrong Gibbs, said: 'There are possibilities here which are rather marvellous. She gave a most wonderful rendering of a difficult song. She is a real contralto with a most artistic conception of the song.' Afterwards he said that her singing, though untutored, had made a tremendous impression on him. The mood was imaginative and very soul-satisfying, whilst the beauty of her voice stood out like a beacon.

About this time, at Workington Presbyterian Church, Kathleen sang in the *Messiah*. Win and her uncle, Albert Murray, neither of whom had heard her sing for some time, were amazed at the development in her voice and realised for the first time some of her potentialities as a singer. They both impressed on her the importance of having lessons. The difficulty was to find the right teacher. Kathleen remembered what Dr. Hutchinson had said and felt sure that he could help. But Dr. Hutchinson was in Newcastle, Kathleen in Silloth, eighty miles away. She wondered how she could have lessons with him.

At this time, in addition to keeping house for her husband, she was giving about twenty piano lessons a week. She felt that money which she earned in this way could justifiably be spent on singing lessons for herself.

When World War II broke out, one of the schools in which Dr. Hutchinson taught music was evacuated to Keswick. He travelled there once a week, and, his route being through Carlisle, was able to give Kathleen lessons.

Of her voice at this time Dr. Hutchinson said: 'Lovely though it was, it was unequal and had one white spot as well as an awkward break between the head and chest registers. The latter proved very stubborn before yielding to treatment and in the course of our weekly lessons we returned to it time and time again. Even when after 18 months I could pronounce it cured, Kathleen would ask me when commencing a lesson and often at its close to "try my break, Doctor". But work went on diligently and persistently until the lovely voice was poised securely throughout its compass—two octaves from bottom G to top G.

'Then we turned our attention to the building of a repertoire. Before she left me, Christmas 1942, she had studied songs by Purcell, Bach's *B Minor Mass*, the *St. John*, the *St. Matthew Passion* and excerpts from the *Choral Cantatas*.

'There were also many of the older Italian arias, all the Handel oratorios—and *The Dream of Gerontius*.

'We worked together for nearly three-and-a-half years. What a joy to direct such gifts, but what a responsibility!'

Her first important engagement after she had begun to take lessons with Dr. Hutchinson was in the Newcastle City Hall on 15th December 1940. All her hopes were centred on it—a performance of the *Messiah*, conducted by Dr. Hutchinson, with a choir of 300 and a full orchestra. The night before the concert she dreamt that the City Hall had been bombed and burnt down, so she set off in a state of almost unbearable anxiety, and when at last she reached Newcastle and found the hall still standing, tears of relief streamed down her face.

CHAPTER FIVE

Frognal

AT the end of 1940, Win, knowing that Kathleen's husband would be called up, obtained a teaching post in Carlisle, so that in due course Kathleen could join her. In those days living conditions were not easy. Another manager would be sent to the bank: the flat over it would have to be vacated. All living space in Silloth, where there was a large aerodrome, was over-crowded.

Fortunately a member of the staff at Win's new school was called up at the same time, and an arrangement was made for the two sisters and their father to rent a small house: so small, according to Kathleen, that she had to open the back door before she could look into the oven. But limited space did not limit happiness. A fruitful period which was to last nearly two years began.

Kathleen took it for granted that she would be responsible for the housekeeping, but it was easier for her now to have her lessons with Dr. Hutchinson and she was able to travel further afield for concerts. She practised singing for hours, steadily building up her repertoire. She welcomed every opportunity to try out the songs she was studying, because she felt that until she had sung them nine or ten times in public, she was not really master of them.

In 1941 she began to keep detailed records of her programmes: she also noted which frock she wore, so that if she went to the same place again, she could dress differently.

A typical programme for this period was:

Handel   *Where'er you Walk*
                Pack Clouds Away

41

Purcell	*Fairest Isle*
	Hark the Echoing Air
Schubert	*The Erl King*
	To Music
	Cradle Song
Vaughan Williams	*Silent Noon*
Bridge	*Go Not Happy Day*
Traditional	*I Have a Bonnet*
	Water Boy

Phyllis Simpson, a music mistress at Carlisle High School, who often played her accompaniments at local concerts, introduced Kathleen to John McKenna during one of his singing tours in Cumberland. He heard Kathleen sing and recommended her to Eve Kisch, who was the 'Music Traveller' of the Council for the Encouragement of Music and the Arts. C.E.M.A. was doing a valuable wartime job in bringing music to people who would otherwise have been out of touch.

After hearing Kathleen sing, Eve Kisch said that there would be plenty of work if she were free to go anywhere at any time. Kathleen replied that she must think it over. At home she discussed it with her sister.

'If I'm away then you'll have to cope with the housekeeping: can I say I'm mobile?' she asked. Win, who had long been urging her to take up a musical career, told her to write immediately and accept whatever engagements were offered. The writing of this letter, June 1941, together with the reversion to the use of her maiden name, marked the beginning of her professional career.

Soon contracts began arriving for C.E.M.A. tours: Kathleen accepted them with great joy. 'Shall never forget my first little C.E.M.A. tour,' she wrote in her diary. 'Three glorious days of music and never a hitch. Maurice Jacobson's accompanying a perfect joy.'

It was to Harry Vincent, C.E.M.A. organiser for a large district in the Potteries that Maurice Jacobson said: 'I've found a star, and I want you to give her whatever engagements you can.'

Eve Kisch was delighted with her protégée and wrote to a

friend, Margot Pacey, 'I have discovered a most promising singer. She is a local girl in Carlisle, with the most glorious contralto voice and with a natural dignity and personality. She's a terrific success with every audience she encounters.' Margot, herself a pianist and accompanist, took the first opportunity to hear Kathleen sing, and later met her in a music studio in Newcastle, where they were to rehearse for a concert.

Afterwards she wrote: 'I felt very much on my mettle as an accompanist and even in those days, when her reputation was as purely local as my own, I felt as I would have felt, had I been playing for Elisabeth Schumann or any other international singer—keyed up to the highest pitch in my anxiety not to let her down.

'I remember playing the *Erl King* for her at one concert and at the end she asked for special applause for the pianist for tackling "the most difficult accompaniment ever written". It was these little personal touches that endeared her so much to audiences.

'She could get away with anything in those days, just as later she could twist the most sophisticated audience round her little finger. I remember her singing some Purcell duets with Helen Anderson and forgetting her words at a certain bar. With complete aplomb she broke off—and apologised. They started again and the same thing happened. Kathleen started to laugh —and soon the hall was in an uproar of amusement. It was the most successful performance of the evening.'

Helen Anderson, who shared many tours with her, said that no matter what conditions they met, nothing seemed to upset Kathleen. The concerts took place in any room that was available: sometimes a barn was used, sometimes a youth club; if there was nowhere else, they even used a chapel. Kathleen occasionally found herself standing in a pulpit—because there was nowhere else where she could be seen—singing *Kitty My Love, will you Marry Me* or *I Have a Bonnet Trimmed with Blue*.

Nothing deterred her, the long journeys, often in the blackout, the uncertainty, the lack of facilities for changing, the various mishaps inseparable from such conditions. Her joy in the work, and in the audience's reaction, were her reward. From an early age she had realised that she must willingly accept the disadvantages of any desired course of action, so she took each day as it came, enjoyed it to the full and made the most of any chance of amusement.

The regional directors of C.E.M.A. had been asked to arrange concerts—out of doors—for people who could only take their holidays at home. It was sometimes difficult to find suitable places. Often they were held in marquees or band stands, and the artists had to cope with typically English weather. On one occasion Tom Harrison, the director of the Midlands region, had the idea of arranging a concert from a punt on the River Trent, where it flows through some public gardens. Kathleen was asked to sing with the Ruth Pearl String Quartet and the flautist John Francis. A programme suitable for such a setting was planned, and as none of Kathleen's folk songs had string accompaniments she scored some of them herself.

On the day of the concert the wind blew so strongly that it almost prevented the flautist from playing at all. Kathleen had to stand between him and the wind, changing her position as the punt moved down the river. Someone had fitted to the punt an outboard motor, but unfortunately the speed could not be regulated, and instead of drifting gently down the river, it panted madly up and down, past the audiences on both banks. Kathleen used to end this story by saying: 'This is the audience—that was.'

She also sang in many schools. The children were usually well behaved and very responsive, but in relation to one concert her diary reads: 'Dreadful kids in the audience—told them off, little brutes.'

About this time, she wrote to the Musical Director of the B.B.C. in Manchester:

Dear Sir,

I have been singing under the auspices of C.E.M.A. for Miss Eve Kisch of Liverpool, the North Western Organiser, and at her request I am writing to ask if I might have an audition in the near future at your studios.

I have had eight broadcasts from Newcastle, but only one since the war began, and I believe that the studios there are now very little used for vocal or instrumental work.

I am a Contralto and include in my repertoire solos by Bach, Handel, Purcell, Schubert, modern English, Lieder, Negro Spirituals, etc. and all oratorios, including Dream of Gerontius, Stabat Mater (Pergolesi), Elijah, Messiah, etc.,

Hoping to receive a favourable reply,
I am,
Yours faithfully,
(Signed) Kathleen Ferrier.

The reply, dated 14th October 1941 was:

Dear Madam,

In reply to your letter of 29th September, auditions of solo performers are not being held at present except in very special circumstances, but as you have broadcast for us a good deal in the past we would be willing to audition you as a singer. It may be some time before members of our Music Department can visit our Newcastle studios, but we will let you know when an audition there would be possible.

Alternatively if you have occasion to visit Manchester we would be very pleased to hear you here, but as we have very few opportunities for offering engagements to solo singers, I do not think it would be worth a special visit.

Yours faithfully,
Maurice Johnstone
Music Director, North Region.

Nothing immediately resulted from her request but she had an engagement to sing in the *Messiah* at St. Annes-on-Sea. Here Alfred Barker heard her and arranged for her to sing with his orchestra in a broadcast from Manchester. She went to St. Annes to rehearse and took the opportunity to hear Dr. Malcolm Sargent conduct the Hallé Orchestra at Blackpool.

After this concert she was introduced by Alfred Barker to Dr. Sargent with the words, 'This girl has a voice'. Dr. Sargent promised to hear her, but he was very busy and it was not until the 21st May 1942, that she sang to him in a Manchester hotel. He told her that he thought she had a great future but that she would find it difficult to get on unless she lived in London.

Notes in her diary about that time say, 'Practising almost all day' or 'Practised for hours'.

Dr. Hutchinson was progressively revealing to her the need for greater technical resource. She for her part had the energy, the singleness of purpose, to put in the many hours of continuous hard practice. Her diary at that time also records the receipt of a letter from Dr. Sargent to say that he would write to Ibbs and Tillett, the well-known concert agents. Ibbs and Tillett acted on Dr. Sargent's suggestion: they arranged an audition in London for an afternoon in July.

Some fourteen years before, Kathleen and her sister had set out from Blackburn to London for Kathleen to play the piano: this time, and in very different circumstances, she was to sing; and this time a decision would be made, vital to her professional career. Together they made their way to Wigmore Hall, in that strange, exciting, dream-like state, born of the memory of having been there before.

But except for Mr. Tillett and Win the Wigmore Hall was empty for the audition. The sisters found it depressing: Win feeling that Mr. Tillett could not possibly judge the quality of a voice in an empty hall; and Kathleen lacking an audience.

On the previous occasion the platform had seemed to sway as she had moved across to the piano. This time she had an accompanist and although she had to stand alone, was not so nervous. She sang a short selection of her songs. At the end Mr. Tillett said that he would put Kathleen's name on his books. Dramatic steps are often characterised by the absence of drama: an hour ago she was a professional singer and now she was a singer with a manager in London.

On the way back to Carlisle she and her sister discussed future plans. Neither of them paused to question the first step: clearly Win must get a teaching post in London, so that she could provide some financial security and moral support, while Kathleen established herself.

From this time opportunity seemed simply to fall into Kathleen's lap. Within a day or two Win had a letter from a colleague who was still teaching in the school where she had been at the beginning of the war. It contained a message from the headmistress. 'Tell her', she said, 'that I need a teacher and I wish she would come back.' And so it was arranged that

Win should move back to London, in time to start the new term after Christmas.

The problem of somewhere to live for father and sisters in war time was again tackled and solved by taking a flat in Hampstead at a rent of £150 per year. There was some reluctance on Kathleen's part because the amount seemed to her to be enormous compared with northern charges.

Feeling that a leaflet with a photograph and press references would help to establish her in London, Kathleen went through all her notices. A recent one from the *Manchester Guardian*—of 21st October 1942—might be helpful!

Miss Kathleen Ferrier, a new singer of remarkable talent, was heard yesterday in the Houldsworth Hall, Manchester. A full, rich contralto voice, flexible throughout its compass and capable of lovely shades of tone and expression, is rare in these days, and as the possessor of such a voice Miss Ferrier is far better equipped by nature than are many contraltos who enjoy considerable fame. And she sings with feeling and intelligence, using her vocal gifts as the servant of her temperament. Miss Ferrier must, however, always be careful to get her words clear. We have just written that her singing can reveal fine tone-shading, but this does not mean that such a result is invariably achieved.

During two or three songs yesterday, the words lost savour and character, and then a sense of monotony was noticed in the actual tonal effect. We may sometimes be tempted, as at this concert, to think that a vocal line can be sustained so beautifully that the words are, after all, of no great importance, but the idea is, of course, a mistaken one. The haziness in diction was not frequent yesterday, and Miss Ferrier is too good an artist to let it go uncorrected on future occasions. Her songs included a group from Brahms and Wolf and some lyrics by English composers.

Granville A. Hill

After much perusal and discussion, the leaflet reproduced between pages 96 and 97, with its quotation from the *Guardian* was printed.

For the removal period Mr. Ferrier went to stay with friends in the north until the Hampstead flat could be made habitable. Win travelled to London to be ready to receive the furniture when it arrived while Kathleen stayed in the north to sing in

Elijah at Runcorn and the *Messiah* in Edinburgh. On this occasion Kathleen stayed with some friends, Mr. and Mrs. Alec Maitland. During the visit, Mrs. Maitland produced an old copy of the Brahms *Four Serious Songs* which she loved. Kathleen tried them through: she sang them over and over again. Mrs. Maitland went out for an hour or two, and when she came back Kathleen was still working at them, enthralled.

On Christmas Eve 1942 the furniture arrived at Frognal Mansions, Hampstead. The remover's men looked up with gloomy resignation at the high building. They toiled slowly up the steep concrete slope, the twenty stone steps to the entrance and the thirty steps to the door of the flat.

There was a large entrance hall, a long lounge with high windows, a big bedroom and a narrow passage, literally as long as a cricket pitch, and with rooms opening on to it like the cabins in a ship. At the far end of the passage was a big square kitchen. The flat certainly presented problems. It was difficult to keep clean and to heat. A draught blew through one's hair as one walked down the passage. It required an enormous amount of carpeting. Curtains, at a time when blackout was essential, were a major undertaking.

Having been brought up in a family where the merits of a job were judged by whether it was safe and whether there was a pension, Kathleen, in coming to London, felt that she had taken a leap in the dark. Under wartime conditions, how could anyone know whether there would be *enough* engagements to justify the step?

CHAPTER SIX

Two Years

KATHLEEN was acutely conscious of being in many ways ill-equipped for concert work on a larger scale. She knew little of the history of music. She had attended very few concerts but had listened a little to the radio. She had seen no first rate opera, heard no Lieder and knew very few works apart from oratorio. Having left school at fourteen, her knowledge of English literature was limited; of foreign languages she knew only a little French and Latin.

On the other hand, she was willing to tackle anything and took for granted that she could learn and learn quickly, whatever she undertook to do. She knew that she had a good voice which had been well developed by Dr. Hutchinson, and that she had the physical strength and vitality essential for a singer. Most important of all, she had an inner compulsion to sing which spurred her on. She could rely on some contracts from C.E.M.A., and she had confidence in her ability to hold an audience.

At the beginning of 1943 she had sung in *Messiah* and *Elijah* and one or two other oratorios. She had also learnt, and sung in public, about forty songs, some classical ones, some Lieder in English, a few negro spirituals and folk songs.

With joy and determination she began to tackle two difficult and exhausting tasks: to make a name for herself as a national artist; and to learn whatever new works she was asked to sing.

She wrote to her old friends in Silloth

My dear Eleanor and Bill,

Having a sit-down—it seems to be the first for many weeks—I am taking the opportunity of writing to you. I wish I could have seen you all before we removed—simply couldn't manage it.

We are more or less settled in—have been in a terrible mess, with painters, electricians, joiners and plumbers. But we're looking posh now!

I made my London debut a week last Monday at the National Gallery and oh boy! did my knees knock! But I got through without running off in the middle or swallowing in the wrong place. Myra Hess, the boss of the concerts—was very nice and encouraging. There was a huge crowd there and it was a bit of a facer, so I was glad when it was safely over.

I'm going up to Edinburgh on Monday for two concerts, then on to Thirsk and Newcastle-on-Tyne and Colne in Lancs. and home again next Monday.

Work is rolling in and I'm pretty well booked up to the end of April, which is just as well with the price of rents!

I'm going on a week's tour in Kent, another round Birmingham, and a 3-weeker in Scotland, so I'm going to be busy.

Do you remember Phyllis Simpson, music teacher at the Carlisle High School? She turned up here the day before the National Gallery concert—she'd come specially to hear it all the way from Cockermouth!

Win and I went to see 'Blithe Spirit' the other day—it was grand. We saw John Clements in the audience. Yesterday I went to the opening of an exhibition of Modern Art—and Jessie Matthews and Cochran were there. Seeing the celebrities, begorra!

Pop and Win send their love to you all and lots of luck for 1943.

Bert[1] is at Bury at the moment and has been made a sergeant and is to stay on there as instructor, so he's near his home and should enjoy life better now.

Lots of love and luck to you all and all at Maryport—Mollie when you see her, and Frances and Tony and all our good pals.

I'll be seeing you, and you've got our address and 'phone number if you're in London, so you've no excuse!

Look after yourselves and let's hear from you when you've a spare minute. Heaps of love. Kath.

Her first fear that she would not get enough work proved groundless, for it often happened that when a concert was over, the organisers booked her again immediately. Her reputation grew, and while travelling she learnt new works. The conditions of those times did not make it easy: trains were crowded, usually

---

[1] Her husband.

with troops who filled the carriages with cigarette smoke; porters were few or non-existent, and Kathleen, who had bought a musquash coat as a protection on cold railway journeys, found after a while that there was a completely bare patch at the side where her suitcase had rubbed against it. Hotels were often cold and uncomfortable and seldom able or willing to provide meals at times convenient to artists: Kathleen would come home and cry out for salads and vegetables, having lived on buns and sandwiches for days at a time.

But home was not always comfortable: domestic help was impossible to find, laundries gave irregular service and heating was always a problem. The flat was equipped with an ancient stove which had a malignant personality. Fed with wartime coke, it either roared away and became almost white hot, or sulked and went out.

Kathleen began to look for a teacher. Realising how easily a voice could be spoiled and knowing how fortunate she was to have had Dr. Hutchinson, she was anxious not to make a mistake. She asked advice from the singers with whom she worked. Some recommended one teacher, some another, and for a time she was undecided.

Kathleen had sung with Roy Henderson at a performance of *Elijah* in Runcorn and had been impressed by his work. After the concert she had said to him, 'How did I do?' and he had replied, 'Your voice is very good, my dear, but you kept your eyes glued to the score. You must learn your work better.' This was the kind of straight talk that Kathleen appreciated, but she told this story somewhat ruefully when she returned home. She decided to ask him to give her lessons.

Kathleen knew she had much to learn. In a light-hearted song she felt free to express her own feelings of gaiety and humour, but if the subject was serious, she was not confident. She had a north country horror of showing emotion, and when she saw someone else 'in a state' she felt unhappy and embarrassed. Roy Henderson in due course helped her to overcome this difficulty. He gave her the assurance of knowing that she was singing well and looking right, thereby freeing her to concentrate all her attention on getting to the heart of a song—of conveying her own feelings about it to the listener.

'Prof.', as Kathleen always called him, became a dear friend of the family and a tower of strength to her. She said that she owed him an incalculable debt for all that he had taught her; she appreciated to the full his unselfish help, his affection and his pride in her as a pupil.

One of the first songs to be learnt was *Che Faro* from Gluck's *Orfeo ed Eurydice*. She sang it for the first time at a recital in Crewe on 10th March 1943. She always loved this music for its strength and its pure classical line. She knew that it suited her. 'It's in the fat of my voice', she once said. Having once sung it publicly, she was emboldened to include it in a recital at Lewes. The occasion was especially important to her because her accompanist was to be Gerald Moore: she was thrilled and overawed at the prospect. Afterwards she said, 'It's a revelation to work with him. *He thinks and breathes with me*'.

At the end of March Kathleen went to Scotland to do a series of C.E.M.A. concerts with Maurice Jacobson and a 'cellist, Kathleen Moorehouse. It was bitterly cold, both in the train and at the concerts, and by the time they reached Aberdeen it was obvious that Kathleen was too ill to go on. Kathleen Moorehouse insisted on calling a doctor, who diagnosed pneumonia and arranged for an ambulance to take her to a nursing home. 'I lay there', wrote Kathleen, 'wondering whether this was the end of my short career as a singer.'

She was ill for three weeks and when she returned home looked thin, pale and very shaky. Before she could hope to do any more work, it was obviously necessary for her to have a holiday. So the two sisters and their father went to a small country hotel at Blindley Heath. Fortunately the weather was good and the fresh air and sunshine began to have effect. Kathleen gradually recovered health and vigour and was able to walk miles in the lovely Surrey countryside.

In the window of a music shop in East Grinstead Kathleen saw some descant recorders. She bought one for Win and one for herself and an instruction book. With due regard for the nerves of the other visitors, they took the recorders out into the open to learn to play them. With many squeaks and involuntary extra notes they practised simple tunes. Kathleen who had just learnt Ivor Gurney's setting of *Down by the Salley Gardens* found that this tune was suited to the recorder's limited compass. She practised until she could play it well: the quiet woods and still country air seemed a perfect setting for the lovely plaintive little tune.

When they went home, Kathleen took up her singing with renewed zest. She wanted to be in very good form for a most important occasion—an engagement to sing in Westminster Abbey. Not only was it the first time that she had sung the *Messiah* in London, it was also the first occasion on which she had worked with Dr. Reginald Jacques. After the rehearsal she admired his authoritative and meticulous reading of the work. It deeply satisfied her desire for truthful interpretation.

The *Times* report of the 18th May 1943 said:

> The soloists were two established Handelians, Miss Isobel Baillie and Mr. William Parsons, and two new-comers, Miss Kathleen Ferrier and Mr. Peter Pears, both of whom established their right to be of that now not very numerous company.

A month later, in a review of recent London concerts in *The Musical Times,* she was delighted to find:

> It remains to give thanks to the performers who most distinguished themselves; to the Griller Quartet, who played Britten's unnecessarily difficult work with great skill; to Frederick Thurston, who joined them in Jacob's Quintet; to the Fleet Street Choir for their contributions to the Belgian concert; and finally to Miss Kathleen Ferrier, who sang the alto part in *Messiah* at Westminster Abbey. I shall not easily forget the natural dignity of her style or the purity of her voice.
>
> Ferruccio Bonavia

Dr. Jacques wrote:

> I shall always remember my first meeting with Kathleen. It was the result of a set of circumstances which I think are worth recording. In the early part of 1943 a trio of well known musicians, a singer, a flautist and a pianist, were touring for C.E.M.A. in the north of England, centred on Newcastle. They were Helen Anderson, John Francis and Harry Isaacs. Helen Anderson was obliged to be

absent from one of the concerts in order to fulfil a lecture engagement, and a local singer was asked to take her place. Miss Kathleen Ferrier arrived for rehearsal, a rather shy girl with a delightful smile.

John Francis told me that he was intending to read a book during the rehearsal, but the moment Kathleen began to sing the book was forgotten, and he sat forward in his chair, completely enthralled by the performance of this unknown artist. After the concert the other soloists told her that in two years' time she would be singing in the Royal Albert Hall in London. This was received by Kathleen with shouts of laughter. But what a true prophecy that was.

This incident was related to me and John Francis asked me to hear Kathleen as 'being something quite special'. I recollect with a qualm that I demurred a little, for as Director of Music to C.E.M.A. I had been listening to hundreds of singers of varying degrees of talent, and I was feeling rather weary of my experience. ('Oh Lord! Another singer', I remember saying, ungraciously.) However, somewhat reluctantly I agreed, and an audition was arranged in London. I was electrified, not only by the natural beauty of her voice, but the glowing sincerity of the whole performance. Kathleen had a way of getting to the heart of the music which was inimitable. Without the slightest hesitation I asked her if she would like to sing in a performance of *Messiah* by the Bach Choir, which was planned to take place in Westminster Abbey the following May. Kathleen was quite incredulous at first, but then said with a radiant smile, 'I'd love to if you think I'll do.' The performance took place on May 17 and was memorable. There was a packed audience of a quality and variety which was typical of London at that time. Soldiers, sailors, airmen, doctors, nurses, civil defence personnel, war-workers of all kinds, *and* the music critics of the great London newspapers who had not heard of Kathleen before. She sang as though inspired and created a very deep impression, and that performance was the first of many engagements with the Bach Choir and myself.

Kathleen was an ideal singer to work with, always cheerful, happy and co-operative wherever we found ourselves together. In the Albert Hall, Westminster Abbey, the Orangery at Hampton Court, at the B.B.C. or in a recording studio. As a singer of Bach's music she had no equal. Quite apart from her own natural talent and training, she must have worked tremendously hard. The lovely long phrases came pouring out, every note accurate in duration (all too rare in the performance of Bach's vocal music, for he so often seemed to forget that singers must breathe!) and making a glorious line, so difficult to achieve, so satisfying to hear.

I believe Kathleen loved singing Bach. She always seemed superbly happy and deeply moved by the music. In the *St. Matthew Passion*, she brought joy and comfort to thousands of people. At the annual performances by the Bach Choir in the Albert Hall, the stillness of those great audiences and the wonderful atmosphere when she was singing, 'Have mercy, Lord, on me' had to be experienced to be believed.

From May 1943, when she first sang in Westminster Abbey, to August the following year, Kathleen learnt and sang for the first time many of the works with which later her name was to become associated. When she was offered an engagement to sing a work unknown to her, she tried it through, accepting if it suited her voice. She relied on being able to learn it by the time the concert was due.

This was a period during which she was finding out which works really suited her. In March 1944 she was asked to sing in a concert performance of *Carmen* at Stourbridge. Feeling that the tessitura was high for her and that she could not really enter into the spirit of the part, she was not particularly keen to learn this work. She made her friends helpless with laughter by demonstrating how she would sing the part, gripping a red rose in the corner of her mouth. However, main parts for contraltos in opera are few, and she must give it a trial. After the concert, however, she was convinced that it was not for her. The report in the *County Express* confirmed this:

Although Miss Ferrier's grave and beautiful contralto is more suited to oratorio than light opera, she enchanted all present with her depth of tone and range of expression in the principal part.

After that she resisted all suggestions that she should sing *Carmen*. Even when Carl Ebert tried to persuade her to play it at Glyndebourne and suggested an interpretation of the part which he felt might be more in accordance with her temperament, she remained firm in her refusal. There were many other works which appealed enormously to her and which she was anxious to sing.

In May 1944 Kathleen had another tour in the Potteries. *The Evening Sentinel,* Hanley, carried the following account of one concert:

> There were two interesting features of the Etruscan Choral Society's concert at the Victoria Hall, Hanley, last night. One was the performance of choir, orchestra and tenor soloist (Peter Pears) of *The Lady of Shalott,* a new work by Maurice Jacobson; the other was the appearance for the second time in the course of a few weeks of Miss Kathleen Ferrier in the dual capacity of contralto soloist and pianist.

In the first half of the concert Kathleen sang two groups of songs and in the second she played the piano part in *The Lady of Shalott,* accompanied by the Newcastle String Orchestra.

Singing in the Potteries always gave her great pleasure. The concerts were well arranged and the audiences appreciative. Most of the concerts were in factories, but when Harry Vincent wanted to arrange for her to give a recital in Victoria Hall, Hanley, which held about two thousand people, she would not let him because she was afraid he would lose money.

There was a great need in that part of the world for a suitable hall for recitals. The Choral Society eventually decided to buy a small hall in a back street in Etruria. They decorated it themselves, and when finished it was delightful, seating 130 people, with an artists' room and a kitchen. It was opened in 1944 by Mary Glasgow, C.B.E., the head of C.E.M.A. Kathleen sang at the opening and Maurice Jacobson accompanied. Kathleen was fond of this hall. 'It's unique and you *must* keep it going', she said, and gave three recitals there without fee. In a short time the hall was paid for. Thus she helped not only to put the concern on its feet financially, but to draw from a radius of more than ten miles the nucleus of an audience which has attended recitals ever since.[1]

Many of the concerts in the Potteries gave Kathleen an opportunity of singing for the first time in public works new to her. Her first performance of Brahms's *Alto Rhapsody* was

[1] This hall is now named after her.

given at Zion Chapel, Silverdale, Staffordshire, with the Etruscan Male Voice Choir.

'Ate, slept, walked and knitted,' reads her diary for a day in June 1943. She was knitting just then because she had sung in a factory which made rubber dinghys. On being shown round afterwards, she had admired the zips which were being used, and the foreman had given her one twenty-five inches long. She was knitting a pullover to fit the zip!

Although putting all her energy into concert work while she was doing it and finding in it great satisfaction, she was always glad to come home. Domestic chores gave relief from the strain of performing. She enjoyed cooking and loved to see at the end of her labours an array of newly baked cakes and buns or a row of shining pots of jelly. Her diary reads on one day: 'Nottingham Theatre Royal, *Elijah*—good performance,' and on the next: 'Home again. Whoopee! Washed, ironed, baked, made jelly. Gorgeous cranberry and apple!'

One day Win brought home a roll of paper about a yard wide and six yards long. She intended to make a frieze to decorate her classroom. The subject was to be the story of the Farmer's Wife, who put her cow up on the thatched roof to graze. Kathleen came in from a rehearsal to find the paper spread out on the kitchen table and Win sketching in the figures. Without waiting to take off her hat Kathleen grabbed a pencil and set to work at the other end of the paper. When the drawing was finished they painted it with bright powder colours. 'Isn't it *satisfying*', said Kathleen. 'I haven't had *enough* painting in my life!

About this time Maurice Codner began to paint her portrait. He had suggested doing it because some of her friends were dissatisfied with the photographs which had been taken for a poster. He thought that the reproduction of a portrait would be more interesting. Kathleen was absorbed in watching him work and said how much she would like to be able to paint in oils, so that she could plaster thick dabs of paint on the canvas. It did not occur to her until much later that she might try.

Whenever she had the opportunity, Kathleen filled in the gaps in her musical education by going to concerts, opera and films. Knowing that Astra Desmond had sung in Elgar's oratorios under the composer himself, she made a point of hearing her in *The Apostles*. She went to hear *Elijah* at the Albert Hall, to Sadlers Wells to see *Hansel and Gretel*; the next day to *The Bartered Bride,* in which she thought Peter Pears was splendid. Some weeks later, at a performance of *The Barber of Seville* she found herself sitting next to Benjamin Britten, whom so far she had not met. 'Gorgeous', says her diary, but whether it referred to *The Barber* or her neighbour is not clear.

Kathleen now found herself singing with well-established artists whose names had been household words in the days when she and her family had attended Celebrity Concerts in Blackburn. Many of them were extraordinarily kind and encouraging to her, notwithstanding that she was now being accorded a large share of the limelight.

She sang in several performances of the *Messiah* with Elsie Suddaby. At a rehearsal Elsie told her, 'I know that you are going right to the top and I want you to have something really good to wear.' And she gave Kathleen a beautiful necklace of amethysts set in silver. This became a most treasured possession, worn on innumerable occasions.

Early in 1944 Kathleen undertook several engagements in place of Astra Desmond, who was ill. One of them was a Tuesday Midday Concert in Manchester. This report was written by the critic who had reviewed her first recital there sixteen months previously :

Manchester Guardian—16th February 1944.

TUESDAY CONCERTS

Owing to sudden illness Miss Astra Desmond could not give the song recital yesterday in the Houldsworth Hall, Manchester, but her place was most worthily filled by Miss Kathleen Ferrier. This was one of several engagements which, at the shortest notice, Miss Ferrier has undertaken for Miss Desmond. Throughout the programme yesterday the soloist showed that she possesses not only a contralto voice of beautiful quality and an unusually flexible and

finely controlled technique but also gifts of expression which are
of a rare kind. The freshness of her style and her abilities in the
matter of characterisation proved that Miss Ferrier brings to her
music a keen intelligence. In quiet, sustained passages she keeps her
words clear without disturbing the legato, and in vigorous rhythmic
songs the smart 'bite' of the consonants adds piquancy.

Granville A. Hill

'Tuppence to speak to me now', said Kathleen. 'Last time he
told me to be careful to get my words clear.'

From that time Astra Desmond took a great interest in Kathleen's career. The following letter, conveying as it did generous
encouragement and appreciation, was much valued and cherished
along with several others received later.

16th February 1944.

Dear Kathleen Ferrier,

I hear you deputised for me in Manchester this week, so it was
with special interest that I listened to you this afternoon.

After hearing your lovely voice and beautiful diction, I know that
you will have compensated easily for any disappointment they may
have felt in Manchester over my non-appearance.

All good luck to you and if a greatly senior singer may be allowed
the liberty! don't let the success you are having and will, I hope,
have yet more abundantly, ever let you cease from studying. I have
seen so many rest on their laurels and then fall by the wayside
when youth begins to fade—the perpetual student lasts ever so
much longer! Forgive this sermon!

With my best wishes,
Yours sincerely,
Astra Desmond

Joan Cross was another artist who was very kind and whose
friendship was highly valued. They first met at a concert in
South Wales where they were singing solos and duets, and Marie
Wilson was playing the violin. The local accompanist was taken
ill and there was no one to take her place. So Kathleen undertook
the accompanying, reading at sight the piano parts for the violin
solos—'very badly, I'm afraid', she put in her diary. Kathleen
enjoyed working with Joan Cross in a broadcast that they did
together in February 1944, when they sang *The Blessed Damozel*

by Debussy. They were to meet again later at Glyndebourne.

In spite of all the travelling, performing and learning that she did, Kathleen never lost a feeling of surprise and wonder that her life had worked out this way. She had not really set out to become a singer: her career had developed through an inner urge that seemed to drive her, an unconscious groping, and a combination of unusual circumstances, some personal and some due to the war.

'You know,' she said, 'if anyone had told me when I was twenty that at thirty-two I should be dashing about the country singing at concerts, I should have laughed my head off. I should have said that no one could make a career in music without going to the Royal Academy or the Royal College, and anyway that it was much too risky a way of earning a living. Now here I am. Fantastico, isn't it?'

Wartime conditions added to this atmosphere of unreality. People lived at high tension and were surprised and, in an odd way, stimulated by finding themselves still alive after a bad raid. 'Still here!' wrote Kathleen in her diary. In one of the periods when raids were frequent there were sometimes as many as thirteen or fourteen people sitting drinking tea in the kitchen of the Frognal flat. There was no air raid shelter in the block of flats which were built on a slope so that, although the lounge windows were some 60 ft. from the ground, it would have been possible on the same floor to climb out of the kitchen windows on to some coal sheds and then to the ground. The kitchen was far from ideal as a shelter. It had two windows and the hot water tank was near the door, but the fact that it was possible to get out, and the thought that the two flats above it would protect it from shell splinters made it seem the best in the circumstances.

Kathleen's friends, the McArthurs, lived on the top floor, so when the raids were bad the McArthurs and their friends and the Ferriers and theirs sat around in the kitchen, cheering themselves with tea and talk. It was not until some months later that Win, going for the first time into the mews behind the flats, glanced up and realised to her horror that the kitchen protruded beyond the flats above and was covered only by a leaded roof.

After some engagements in the north, Kathleen returned with two precious lengths of material given by a friend and she and Win each decided to make a dress. They began to cut them out, but every few minutes along came another flying bomb, and they had to drop tools, run into the corridor and lie flat until they heard it land. 'I'm fed up with this "Oh Allah" business', said Kathleen. 'Thank goodness our father is in Blackburn. I know what we'll do. I have to be in Durham next week. Let's go now and have a peaceful week there!' The next day they were on their way north.

The following week was a memorable oasis of peace and quiet happiness. The weather was perfect. Each morning they took out a punt, paddled it along through the coal black waters of the Tees until they found a secluded spot. Then while Win held the copy and prompted, Kathleen sang through her part of the Angel in *The Dream of Gerontius*. Roy Henderson had told her that, until she could sing it from memory, she could not hope to interpret the part well, and she knew this to be true. During that week she learnt most of it.

By good fortune she was also able to rehearse the Brahms *Serious Songs* with her one-time accompanist, Margot Pacey, who was by then living in Durham with her husband and son, Johnny, who was six weeks old. Each evening Kathleen and Win walked up South Street to the Pacey's house which must surely have one of the most wonderful views in England—the front of Durham Cathedral. While Win sat and watched as the setting sun sent changing light on to the warm red stone of the cathedral, Kathleen and Margot practised the Brahms *Serious Songs*. They were both greatly moved by them, and at the end of *Oh Death how bitter art thou,* they were sometimes both in tears. Then Kathleen would begin to laugh to relieve the tension. She would sit down at the piano and perform a silly monologue called *The Three Trees.* Then she would urge Margot and Jack to play her favourite flute solo, a delightful little composition of Margot's, called *At the sign of the Red Bull.*

After a holiday in Durham, Kathleen had two engagements—one in Liverpool, the other a broadcast from Manchester—to sing Brahms's *Four Serious Songs.*

With the increase in repertoire came the horror of forgetting her words. It was bad enough in recitals when the audience's attention was concentrated on her. But it was a nightmare to her in works where a slip on her part might have brought the whole performance, orchestra, choir and conductor to a standstill. This was particularly applicable to *The Dream of Gerontius*. 'I never draw an easy breath till it's over', she said.

Gradually she found out by experience the things that tended to make her forget her words: programme rustlers, people who coughed, a person in the audience wearing something arresting. She said that it was a disadvantage to have such good sight that she could see members of the audience clearly right to the back of the concert hall. When she had a headache, singing was so painful from the physical effort and the 'pressure of the sound' that she felt as though her head rocked from side to side, but she could not take an aspirin for fear that it would make her forget the words.

'There's one small comfort', she said: 'if I forget a word, I *usually* find something fairly sensible to put in its place.' The way she said 'usually' indicated her concern. She had to tell the following story a number of times in order to help herself to face her fears.

'At Silloth, before the war, I was singing *Where'er you Walk*, and as I got to the part "Where'er you turn your eyes", my mind went a complete blank and I sang the first thing that came into my head—"Where'er they eat the grass". Then, having started, I had to repeat it: "Where'er they eat the grass", "Where'er they eat the grass". Was my face red!' and she added as an after-thought, 'It's sometimes a bit awkward when the audience *can* hear the words!'

The first two years in London were characterised by consolidation of a few already familiar oratorios and the learning and performing for the first time of many works new to her. These included Handel's *Judas Maccabaeus* and *Samson*; Bach's *St. Matthew Passion, St. John Passion, Christmas Oratorio* and *Mass in B Minor*; Mendelssohn's *Elijah*; Dvorak's *Requiem*; Elgar's *The Kingdom* and Vaughan Williams's *Mass in G*.

She also took part in *The Blessed Damozel* and a concert performance of *Merrie England*. She gave a performance of the *Four Serious Songs* in Liverpool in 1944 and a second performance in Manchester was broadcast. For both, the transcription for orchestra was by Dr. Malcolm Sargent, who also conducted. In singing this, the *Alto Rhapsody* and *Frauenliebe und Leben* she began to explore territories and languages new to her.

By the end of 1944 it became clear that a further stage in her career had been passed. She was in demand by a large and increasing public; she was recognised by colleagues and critics as 'In the front rank of contemporary contraltos'; she was being asked to broadcast; she had a contract to make gramophone records; she had engagements booked for as far as a year ahead; she had the technique, the growing repertoire, the experience and the assured future that now balanced caution with confidence.

And so in two years of intensive effort her first tasks were accomplished: her repertoire was considerably increased, and she had acquired the status of an artist of national repute.

CHAPTER SEVEN

A Singer's Life

A PERSON may be taught how to sing, but there is no training for *living the life of a singer*. Each artist must face and cope personally with a number of inevitable problems—physical, psychological and musical—which always remain, and which loom especially large during the consolidation of a high reputation.

These problems do not appear successively: they cannot be dealt with in turn. They form an entire front, requiring attention, energy and thought, in order that a workable pattern of life can be achieved. For Kathleen, they related to clothes, an increased number of engagements, learning and rehearsing facilities, broadcasting and the new field of gramophone recording. In addition to all these there was in the back of her mind the problem of the future of her marriage, a problem which, though shelved for the moment, would have to be faced when the war ended.

The development of an artist may well depend on the successful tackling of such problems.

Clothes play an important part in a woman singer's life. Badly fitting garments, jangling ornaments, swinging earrings cause discomfort and defeat concentration; but the consciousness of being well dressed promotes high morale; unbecoming dresses can be irritating and distracting to an audience, but enjoyment is increased if the performer makes a pleasing picture on the stage.

In the days of clothing coupons there were very few evening dresses. Kathleen was chary of buying ready-made ones, having had the embarrassing experience of appearing on a platform wearing a similar dress to the soprano's. Clearly she must have her things specially made; but who was to do it? Win tentatively offered to try. Since the days when she helped her mother to make clothes for college, she had always made some of her own, but it was a very different matter to produce dresses suitable for concert wear. However, she set to work and made several which Kathleen liked and wore frequently. A peacock-green Liberty furnishing brocade with a Chinese pattern of dull gold and orange made a useful evening dress. Not only was it comfortable to wear, but it packed without creasing, and Kathleen wore it for several years, taking it twice to America.

When the war ended, Win urged her to go to a first-rate shop and buy at least one really good model dress. Feeling by this time more secure about her career, Kathleen bought a beautiful turquoise velvet gown with a muff of the same material. 'Well, I've paid the earth for it,' she said, 'but at any rate I shan't meet a soprano wearing the identical dress!' The next day, passing the same shop, she glanced into the window and saw, beautifully displayed and complete with muff, the same dress in *pink* velvet! Soon after this, a young dressmaker, John Michael, who was beginning to build up his career after the war, was introduced to her. She liked him and his work, and from that time he made most of her clothes.

Although she was generous in giving presents to other people, Kathleen resisted the temptation to spend much money on herself. When she did buy something which seemed to her extravagant, she came home feeling guilty and seeking reassurance. Running in one day from a concert in Lancashire, she burst out, 'Oh, I've done a terrible thing. I met a woman whose husband had just died and she needed some ready money. She offered to sell me her squirrel coat. I bought it—I do need a new coat, don't I?'

Occasionally she felt justified in buying some luxury. Wandering round Manchester one morning after a concert, she saw a lovely handbag in a shop window. After looking at it for some time she decided that it was too expensive and, putting temptation firmly behind her, walked away back to the hotel.

c

But after reading the notices of her concert, she decided that she had 'earned a treat', so back she went to the shop and bought the bag!

Compared with a year or so ago there were twice as many engagements to fulfil and travelling was still difficult and uncomfortable. Needing to avoid fatigue and hoping to be able to learn in the train, Kathleen now began to take first-class tickets. The shortage of taxis and the reluctance of taxi drivers to go long distances forced her to develop a persuasive technique. 'I suppose you couldn't possibly manage to take me to Hampstead', she would say wistfully to the glum-looking taxi driver at Euston. 'I'll make it worth your while.' Usually it worked.

After one or two experiences of 'hospitality' which were irritating and exhausting—inconsiderate people who insisted on her singing for them *after* a concert, or kept her up late—she accepted offers only from people who she knew realised her need for peace and comfort.

In June 1945, when the war in Europe had just ended, she went to Stoke to give a series of concerts in factories, along with a cellist, Douglas Cameron, and an accompanist whom she had not met, Phyllis Spurr. The tour went very well and at the end of the week Kathleen, who was looking out for a good accompanist to take with her on tour, decided that Phyllis was just the sort of person that she needed. This was the beginning of an association which was a great joy to both. In the years that followed Phyllis played for many of Kathleen's concerts. She toured with her, accompanied at recording sessions and went with her to lessons with Roy Henderson. Phyllis was always ready to come to the flat at Frognal and spend as much time in rehearsing as Kathleen wanted.

During those years she was always learning and often needed Phyllis's help. Even if the work was in manuscript, Kathleen insisted on sight-reading it straight through with the accompanist so as to get a general idea. She would sit at the treble end of the piano singing her part, striking a note occasionally to help herself with a difficult entry or interval. When she had a clear conception of the work, Kathleen would then

practise alone, sitting at the piano and playing the accompaniment
herself until she was ready to memorise. In trains and buses, as
she travelled about, she would learn it by heart. Her friend Ena
Mitchell, walking along the corridor of a train, glanced into a
compartment and saw Kathleen singing away, completely
absorbed. Ena watched her for some time, but Kathleen remained
unconscious of her surroundings.

When the words were known, Phyllis came in again to play
the accompaniment, so that Kathleen could turn away from the
piano and learn to rely on her memory. They usually worked
with intense concentration for about one and a half hours, then
there would be a break for a cup of tea, a chat and a joke, then
back for another hour and a half. As well as learning, Kathleen
was always rehearsing the pieces that she knew, in an endeavour
to perfect them. She never sang anything in public without
rehearsing beforehand—even the solos in the *Messiah*.

The absence of an audience when she broadcast meant that
she could take off her shoes and feel the solid floor beneath her;
she could also move her hands freely, but the dryness caused
by the studio atmosphere sometimes produced a 'frog in the
throat', and the realisation of the enormous size of the audience
and the clarity with which the microphone would reveal im-
perfections caused her considerable nervous tension.

On one occasion she was anxious to hear one of her programmes which was being broadcast while she was travelling.
She took a portable wireless with her, but the noise of the train
made listening impossible; she did not try it again.

In 1944, Kathleen began to make gramophone records for
Columbia. For her first she chose two songs by Maurice Greene,
a contemporary of Handel, *O Praise the Lord* and *I will lay me
down in Peace*. Having sung them frequently at concerts and feeling
at ease with them, they seemed to be a sensible choice.

The record arrived home in due course, and when it was
played she listened to it with growing disappointment and alarm.
Never before having heard her own voice recorded, she could
not judge whether the reproduction was true or not and was
worried by a hardness of tone which was particularly marked in
the louder passages. Was there a hard edge to her voice which,

while not noticeable in a concert hall, showed up on a record? Or was the explanation that hers was a voice which was unsuitable for recording? In either case it was worrying. It was a great relief to read therefore in the *Gramophone* of November 1944:

> Kathleen Ferrier, besides having a beautiful voice, even throughout, possesses a sense of the value of words, and her soft singing of the end of *I will lay me down in Peace* is very moving. Being perhaps, rather too near the microphone, her tone in the vigorous *O Praise the Lord* has a little edge on it which does not really belong to her voice. The balance is fairly good.

In April 1945, the second record was made. Two songs from Handel's opera *Ottone* were chosen. Of a suitable length, they made a good contrast: *Spring is Coming* being joyous, and the other, *Come to me Soothing Sleep* quiet and peaceful.

Kathleen enjoyed singing them, and although again she was disappointed on first hearing the record, she felt that it was a slight improvement on the previous attempt. Later however, she laughed at the over-emphatic way in which she repeated the phrase 'Spring is coming'. 'If I'd syncopated it as well', she said, 'it would have made a happy little jazz number.' She proceeded to show how it would go when sung in syncopated rhythm with the appropriate foot tappings and movements of the arms.

The review of this record, however, written by Alec Robertson in the *Gramophone* of June 1945 encouraged her:

> The two airs sung by Miss Ferrier are sharply contrasted. The first one here entitled *Spring is coming* comes from Act I, and begins 'La speranza e giunto in porto' (literally, 'Hope has come into Harbour'). It is full of joy. The other one, from the fourth scene of Act II, begins 'Vieni o figlio caro mi consola' ('Come, dear son, and comfort me'). It is in Handel's consolatory key of E major. Both airs are sung by Gismonda, widow of the tyrant of Italy, Berengaria. Gismonda is a soprano, Ottone the hero, is the contralto part in the opera. It will be seen that both the 'translations' and the casting are at fault if we look at the matter with critical rectitude. I remain grateful, however, for being given this lovely music so beautifully sung and accompanied. The balance is perfect and the recording is amazingly true to life. Miss Ferrier's rich tones were not fully revealed in her previous disc. I have only one small

criticism. She gives too much weight of tone to the highest notes in the 'sleep' song and the tranquil vocal line is thereby disturbed. There are many fine contralto songs in the Handel operas— Senesino and Carestini were both artificial contraltos—and also, of course, in the oratorios. Please, Miss Ferrier, give us any number of these, with their rightful orchestral accompaniment, and if not in the original Italian—in the case of the operas—then at least in translations which have some relation to the proper meaning.

In February 1946, Kathleen began recording for Decca and, except for Mahler's *Kindertotenlieder* and two duets with Isobel Baillie, she recorded in future exclusively for that company.

Although in time she grew more used to recording, it was always one of her most difficult tasks. Listening to her own records also remained a painful and chastening experience. Although full of admiration for the technical achievements of the recording engineers, her *own* performances fell so far short of the supremely high standard she set herself that, had it been possible, she would have remade almost all her records.

The records of the Brahms *Alto Rhapsody* seemed to her quite good and there were parts of the *St. Matthew Passion* records which pleased her. One or two of the folk songs were 'not too bad, either'.

Gradually she made adequate adjustments to a new and much more intense way of living: she became free to put into her singing the whole force of her personality. It is not surprising then, that she should reach a higher level both in the number and in the quality of her performances. In the month of December 1945 she gave three recitals, a performance of *Elijah* and sang the *Messiah* seventeen times. All this involved staying in nineteen different places and travelling over two thousand miles.

The Times, in a report of the *St. Matthew Passion* conducted by Dr. Jacques, on 19th March 1945, said: 'Bach, who loved the contralto voice, would surely have approved Miss Kathleen Ferrier's noble singing of the meditative arias.'

On September 15th 1945, she sang *L'Air des Adieux* from Tschaikowsky's opera *Joan of Arc* at a Promenade Concert. It was broadcast, the estimated number of listeners being five million. Of this performance Julius Harrison wrote in the *Sunday Times*:

> Kathleen Ferrier proved that England can still produce voices of an international order.

CHAPTER EIGHT

Top A

DURING the war Mr. and Mrs. John Christie had used the famous opera house at Glyndebourne as a children's home: for seven years there had been no performances. By the end of the war it was clear that an increasing number of people were listening to serious music. Symphony concerts were crowded—young people forming a significant portion of the audiences. Recitals were well attended; opera was evoking new widespread interest. In 1945 Benjamin Britten, whose first opera *Peter Grimes* had deeply affected many people, was at work on a second. It was to be called *The Rape of Lucretia* and plans were in hand to produce it at Glyndebourne.

Kathleen's name was suggested for the part of the Roman matron, Lucretia. Benjamin Britten enthusiastically supported the idea. He had heard her sing in a performance of the *Messiah* in Westminster Abbey and 'was impressed immediately by the nobility and beauty of her presence, and by the warmth and deep range of her voice'.

It was Peter Pears who suggested to Kathleen herself that she should play the name part in the new opera. For a short time she was undecided. Hitherto she had found no contralto operatic roles which appealed to her. She was, naturally enough, flattered by such an offer but nervous about taking the chief part without any previous experience of stage work.

Before the war the audience at Glyndebourne had been international. It seemed likely that a successful appearance there would bring her name before a much wider public than she had so far reached. It was a challenge and an opportunity which she found

71

it hard to resist. After hearing the story of the opera and being assured that there would be a long period of rehearsal, she agreed to take the part.

The rehearsal period at Glyndebourne was memorable: the stimulation of working with other keen musicians on a new project; the anxiety about acting; the joy of living in beautiful surroundings; the emotional strain of learning to play a moving and tragic part; and above all the struggle to achieve a professional standard of acting.

Acting indeed presented by far the most difficult problem, but when she was almost in despair, Joan Cross came to the rescue. With patience and kind understanding she taught Kathleen how to move on a stage and how to make gestures which looked natural and easy. Having practised, watched the others and mastered some basic techniques, the next task was to build up a conception of the part.

The first act presented no intractable problem. The lovely, peaceful music, the quiet dignified role, was something into which Kathleen could enter without reservation. But the confession and suicide in the second act she found almost unbearably moving and it took her some time to gain enough control over her emotions to be able to portray the part at all.

Conscious of her inexperience, she was above all afraid of appearing amateurish. As rehearsals progressed some of her fears were lulled, but she was anxious about the opening performance. All was well however: the dreaded second act went without a hitch and the 'first night' ended successfully.

Under the title of 'My First Opera' Kathleen broadcast in 1948 some of her thoughts and experiences.

'In a bus one evening, going back to our hotel after a performance of the *Messiah* I was told the story of the second opera which Benjamin Britten proposed writing—*The Rape of Lucretia*. It sounded fascinating. At the end of the description I was asked if I would consider singing the part of Lucretia. Heavens! what thoughts raced through my mind. Could I even *walk* on a stage without falling over my own rather large feet, not to mention having to sing at the same time—that is, of course, if I could ever *learn the music*! (I had heard two performances of *Peter*

Grimes and had metaphorically taken off my hat to the singers who had succeeded in learning this wonderful but difficult work.)

'It was to be at Glyndebourne—that most lovely opera house situated on the Sussex Downs—and in the late spring when I wasn't busy. To be able to stay in one place for six weeks or two months, to be able to unpack and keep things in drawers instead of suitcases, to have regular meals instead of a succession of excruciatingly dull sandwiches: my mind was made up. I would learn that music if it was the last thing I did.

'The opera still had to be composed, but by April of 1946 the first pages began to come in, and it was *printed,* thank goodness, and completely legible. What a relief!

'It was lovely, peaceful and most beautiful and as I studied and memorised it, it became simple. The second act was very different and there was terror, sorrow, hysteria and suicide with which to cope. But with the help of my accompanist, and after much hard work on railway journeys, I learned each portion of the work as it came through.

'Being fitted for the gowns was a new experience; and I never found standing for about two hours exhausting. I was much too interested in seeing John Piper's wonderful designs being made up in lovely materials. From a gown fitting I would dash to a wig fitting. The first sight of my wig gave me the surprise of my life. To give the impression of a sculptured head it was made of papier-mâché curls stitched on to the lining, reaching to my shoulder blades and dyed black. It was hard and headache-making, and while wearing it I wouldn't be able to raise my eyebrows to get a top note, no matter how hard I tried.

'It had been decided to have a double cast, to avoid singers becoming tired. One day in May we all met at Lewes station and were taken in omnibuses to Glyndebourne. We were greeted by the owner of the opera house and his wife—Mr. and Mrs. Christie—and became guests in their wonderful Elizabethan home to which the opera house is attached. We were shown to our rooms in which flowers had been arranged to greet us. It was exciting, unbelievable and wonderful—and oh, the view from my window—a real time-waster!

'After we had settled down and unpacked, notices were

posted on various doors about rehearsals. Until this time each singer had only had his own part; but now they began to fit together like a jigsaw puzzle. Long before we made acquaintance with the stage, we all knew the music well and I, for one, was terribly anxious to get going, with what I knew would feel and look like seven-leagued feet and arms!

'We had much time off when we weren't rehearsing. A singer is lucky in this respect: he or she just can't work all day, or the vocal cords will go on strike. Talking, too—that I find the worst thing in the world for the voice. Perhaps I speak somewhere at the back of my neck, instead of on the mask of the face, and being feminine probably do too much of it, anyway.

'Sometimes in the evenings we would play tennis, knit furiously or sing madrigals in one of the lovely rooms of the house. Bright yellow socks I remember growing apace with every hour. And on red-letter days trips to Brighton in an open car and a browse round the old junk shops. A real holiday after months of living in trains and not always hospitable hotels!

'When the work was getting knit together there was not so much free time—we were all wanted more often to walk the boards. I remember my first day trying to walk only a few steps in a pair of heel-less shoes which flapped like a tap-dancer's as I moved or curtsied. *That* was a mistake I didn't repeat.

'This first day let me down lightly. I was sitting most of the time, anyway, but I couldn't believe how difficult it was just to do the simplest arm movements without feeling like a broken-down windmill. I used to practise them everywhere, on the lawn, in my room, for hours in front of a mirror, and watch other people's gestures when they were acting and when they weren't. It was hard going and I was an embarrassed beginner.

'I was helped *enormously* by the other singers. They could have been very intolerant of my inexperience and impatient of my readiness to giggle or cry—one just as easy as the other—but they gave me tips and advice and encouragement for which I can never be grateful enough. I found the second act *so* moving that I went round the place with a permanent lump in my throat, and was relieved when rehearsals were over and I could breathe again till next day.

'About the only other time I had been on a stage was at school, as Bottom in *A Midsummer Night's Dream*, which is rather a far cry to the tragic *Lucretia*. Of course to do the job really properly I should have had lessons in deportment, acting and make-up, but this is a branch of art which it seems has, until just recently, been neglected by opera singers—in this country at least. (I am so glad to hear of an opera school which has been formed here in London for speech, acting, deportment and interpretation, and which I hope will thrive and produce singers who can make an opera as convincing as an actor or actress can a play. Good luck to Miss Joan Cross, who has had the brains, courage and unselfishness to make this a tangible reality out of a dream.)

'The dress rehearsal came. Through an unsuccessful struggle to change gowns and shoes in about four minutes, I missed an entry. Then, having stabbed myself, I fell like a hard-baked dinner roll. After this I thought it was time I shuffled off this mortal coil and did an Ophelia-like exit into the lake with only a belligerent swan for company. Whattalife! Oh for a peaceful *Messiah*!

'I was given more instructions and help, and by the time the first night came along was feeling a little better. Apart from the fact that my wig stuck on my shoulder pads every time I turned my head and I had to free it with a series of jerks, nothing went very wrong for the rest of that memorable evening.'

Hans Oppenheim, associate conductor, wrote:

My first work with Kathleen was on *Lucretia* in 1946, when I was in charge of musical studies for the very first performance of the opera. She came every day to our flat in Bina Gardens, overjoyed at the beauty of the music, but very anxious because of her complete lack of stage experience. The style of Britten's music too was new to her who at that time had mainly concentrated on oratorio work and English songs, written by a previous generation of composers. But her grasp of the musical and technical difficulties of the score as well as the psychological problems of the part was almost immediate. And then began the never-to-be-forgotten time of rehearsals at Glyndebourne.

If I remember right we had five weeks of complete concentration on this work. I have never taken part in any musical preparation which involved anything like the emotional strain which the whole company, without exception, experienced, nor in any comparable bliss as we began to explore the magic of this opera, which slowly came to life, musically and scenically. I can still see those two radiant creatures, Kathleen and Nancy Evans, the other Lucretia, both the best of friends, trying to help one another over their different difficulties.

The actual dying while having to sing a set of phrases covering the complete compass of her voice, gave Kathleen a good deal of trouble. At that time she got a great deal of help from Joan Cross 'behind the scenes' as it were. 'I don't know what to do with my feet', Kathleen used to complain. But the steady patience and understanding from the producer, Eric Crozier, gave her confidence, and so, on the day of the first night, only a handful of people might have realised that Kathleen had been for the first time on a professional stage. Later, on tour in the provinces and in Holland, I had the good fortune to conduct a number of performances of this opera, and rarely if ever was one reminded of a singer struggling with a set of entirely new problems for the first time: gestures, movements, keeping contact with the conductor while acting, mastering vocal difficulties in awkward positions and so on.

'When will they give me a comic part to sing?' she complained quite often, and she meant it. Alas, she never got the chance.

Benjamin Britten wrote:[1]

Many performances of the work were given that summer and autumn: two weeks (if I remember rightly) in Glyndebourne, then a tour of the provinces, with a week each in Manchester, Liverpool, Edinburgh, Glasgow and Oxford, and a season of two weeks back in London at Sadler's Wells Theatre. All this time Kathleen's Lucretia grew steadily in stature, always vocally richer, and her acting more relaxed, until it became one of the most memorable of contemporary opera creations. She was always least happy about the 'hysterics' I mentioned before, partly because it was the least close to her own nature, and the part was in *tessitura* very high for her. One note at the climax, a top A, was quite out of her reach, so I wrote her an *ossia* of an F sharp. At one of the last performances at Glyndebourne, listening from the side of the stage, I was startled to hear her let out a ringing top A. Afterwards she confessed that she had got excited, forgotten her caution, and the F sharp, and

[1] *Kathleen Ferrier: A Memoir.* Hamish Hamilton.

was equally startled to hear herself singing an A (the first she had ever sung in public, I think I remember her saying). After that it was always the A, and I crossed the F sharp out of the score.

Kathleen played the part of Lucretia many times. There were probably not many people who realised what it demanded of her. Few penetrated her defences or saw through the face she showed the world and perhaps none saw far.

> 'Last night Tarquinius ravished me
> And took his peace from me...'

In this opera to sing these words demands a high order of emotional control, but when their meaning has personal significance, the strain can be almost intolerable.

Perhaps the real explanation of that 'Top A' lies in its symbolic revelation of how she dealt with the deep problems of her life.

[1] The above extract from *The Rape of Lucretia*, libretto by Ronald Duncan, music by Benjamin Britten, is reproduced by kind permission of Boosey and Hawkes Ltd.

CHAPTER NINE

Edinburgh

Amsterdam
30th September 1946.

Dearest Both,

Arrived all in one piece, and enjoyed every minute. The boat lurched a bit—trying to avoid fog I understand. The sea was as smooth as a millpond—no casualties—and we were on time all the way. We had been huddled all together in a dormitory cabin—about twelve of us, but Joan, Nancy and I asked for and achieved cabins, which was much better. Peter Diamand—Dutch agent—met us at the Hook and we went by train from there through Rotterdam, Haarlem to Amsterdam. The cleanest houses and windows you ever did see and flowers in the fields all the way. Ben, Peter and Eric met us at Amsterdam with a bouquet of roses for all the girls—mine are twenty yellow ones—absolutely gorgeous—and we had a hilarious journey in a bus to this hotel which is *very* nice.

I have a room on the first floor with *balcony* with chairs and table outside! We had a magnificent lunch of beefsteak—real undercut—peas and fried potatoes and gâteaux and red wine—then I slept for a bit and had a walk round Amsterdam with the gang. It's a most lovely city with beautiful canals down every side street and lovely big-windowed tall houses. We had tea in a little cafe and had fun pointing out which cake we wanted and Ben couldn't reckon up his change at all—guilders and cents! Peter's good at mime and was a riot with the waitress. Now we're all going out for some dinner—then I'm going straight to bed to recover from only about three hours sleep last night.

Peter has a sore throat, but expect he'll be all right on the night! Everything absolutely grand and my eyes popping out with excitement! Wish you were here too. Loads of love,

Kath.

Of course her eyes were 'popping out with excitement': first venture into opera, first visit to Holland, indeed first time *ever* that she had been abroad.

The Dutch audiences were enthusiastic about the *Rape of Lucretia* and Peter Diamand immediately asked how soon Kathleen would be able to return and give recitals.

When the run of the opera in Holland ended, Kathleen took a short holiday in Denmark, staying with Mr. and Mrs Aksel Schiotz and their family. In the preface to the Danish edition of the *Memoir* Aksel Schiotz wrote: 'During her short stay in Copenhagen she became a close and true friend, who shared happiness and sorrow with us and took the children to her heart with a motherly tenderness that was part of her nature.'

On the 1st November 1946 she came home. By this time an important decision about her marriage had been made. Early in 1947 she applied for and in March of that year obtained annulment of her marriage.

She came home also to face a period of six months' very strenuous work. Back to living in suitcases: back to the daily packing and unpacking, uncomfortable railway journeys, sleeping in a different bed almost every night, inadequate meals, lack of freedom inseparable from living in hotels, constant necessity for adapting oneself to different concert halls and fresh colleagues. Above all back to the overriding compulsion to perform at a certain time whether one felt capable of it or not.

It was only when she was very tired that Kathleen 'wondered whether it was worth it'. Usually the satisfaction of singing well, the thrill of the music and the warmth of the audience's reception were ample reward.

The fear felt years before had been that she might not get enough contracts. But now began a long period of overwork. It seemed impossible to avoid. Not only was it difficult to refuse a request, especially when people asked her personally, but often the most interesting dates came when others had already been arranged. Having once promised to appear, she never cancelled a concert, somehow managing to fit them all in.

The miscellaneous and the Celebrity concerts in which she sang a group of songs such as *Che Faro, Art Thou Troubled, Pack*

Clouds Away, Sigh No More, Star Candles and *Bold Unbiddable Child* continued, but their number diminished, recitals taking their place. In 1947, came her first visit to Ireland, when she gave two recitals in the Great Hall of Queen's University, Belfast. 'By the time I'd finished I'd sung practically everything I knew, including Brahms's *Four Serious Songs* and a group of Schubert Lieder in German. I simply must learn more Lieder.' And so, at Prof's suggestion, whenever her engagements permitted, she arranged to go for coaching to Hans Oppenheim, who later wrote:

In our work she gave herself up entirely and unquestioningly to my suggestions. We had a standing agreement: she would listen to every advice given to her, try it out, and only if she found after a while that she could not make it her own, she would discard it. But there was never any attempt at arguing. Even after the musical world was at her feet she remained in her preparatory work the devoted student, modest, keen and untiring.

Often my embarrassment was acute when K. asked me to translate a Lied to her literally and I realised only then how many of these words are cheap, commonplace and used to adorn emotions which it would have been difficult to be in sympathy with but for the beautiful music, for which they served as pegs. Schubert, Brahms and Mahler were the main objects of Kathleen's studies. Soon she developed a passion for Mahler, who often moved her to tears.

I do not think that Kathleen had crossed the Channel before she went to Holland. So the German idiom was really foreign to her beyond any difficulties created by the language. As she rose to fame and toured the world she acquired gradually the sense of style which plays so vital a part in any interpretation but particularly in Lieder singing.

*   *   *

It was at the house of Mr. and Mrs. Hamish Hamilton, through the introduction of Rudolf Bing, that Kathleen first sang for Bruno Walter. He had been invited to conduct Mahler's *Das Lied von der Erde* (*Song of the Earth*) at the first Edinburgh Festival in 1947 and was searching for a contralto to take part in it.

Of this meeting Bruno Walter said: 'I asked her to sing Lieder by Brahms and, I believe, by Schubert; after these I begged her to try also some lines of the *Song of the Earth*, which she did not know. She overcame their great difficulties with the ease of the born musician, and I recognised with delight that here was potentially one of the greatest singers of our time; a voice of rare beauty, a natural production of tone, a genuine warmth of expression, an innate understanding of the musical phrase—a personality.

'From this hour began a musical association which resulted in some of the happiest experiences of my life as a musician.'

The association was for Kathleen too, one of the happiest and most inspiring of her life. The engagement to sing in *Das Lied von der Erde* under Bruno Walter's direction presented a challenge: the type of music had not hitherto been tackled; it was the first full-length work in German; it was the first Edinburgh Festival; and she felt Bruno Walter set a standard that would be very difficult for her to achieve.

But there was also another full-scale work to be learnt. She was already engaged to play *Orfeo* at Glyndebourne in June 1947. The opera was to be performed in Italian, so she began to have Italian lessons from Alfonso Gibilaro and to learn the part. In a few days at home between a performance of *The Dream of Gerontius* at the Albert Hall and *St. Matthew Passion* at Southwark Cathedral, she went for coaching. In the train between recitals at Leeds and Bolton, Liverpool and Nottingham, she worked at the part. On the 12th May the rehearsals began at Glyndebourne.

Again, as in the previous year, there was the relief of staying in one place, and a beautiful one, for several weeks, the joy of living with congenial people, the effort to learn a long and difficult role, and the feeling of inadequacy about her acting. On this occasion however, there was no difficulty about the wig. Her own hair was cut short and Ann Ayars, the American taking the part of Euridice, set it for her before each performance so that it lay in flat curls close to her head.

To her old Silloth friend, Frances Bragg, she wrote:

Until Tuesday morning I hadn't had a single free minute—I'd been cleaning my teeth with soap for days because I hadn't had time to go into Lewes for some toothpaste. I am doing *Orfeo* here with an American Euridice, a Greek God of Love, a German producer and conductor and an Italian coach. Talk about the Tower of Babel! It is all in Italian and you can guess the job I'm having to learn the words from memory. I was so pleased with myself because I'd memorised two acts whilst travelling, but when I arrived here much of it was changed. I've cried for three days!

A few days later she wrote home:

Just to let you know I'm still in one piece, and hope you are too. The stage manager has brought me a lyre of heavy plywood to get used to carrying it, and it's going to make a lovely weapon when the conductor tries me too far. One of these days he won't know what's hit him! He still shrugs his shoulders in despair, calls me an oratorio singer, and shouts himself hoarse. He was vaccinated yesterday, so heaven help me in a day or two when his temp. goes up! I wish I didn't cry so easily. *I* can shout too. The Italian is a poppet and has helped me very much—we've had a good laugh or two, because he gets mixed up in bitch and beach! The Christies are pets, the food very good and the weather lovely. I've been to bed each night after dinner to alter my score—stick bits in and take bits out—and have been doing about fourteen hours a day, but last night I went to the local with the stage manager and had a dirty big pint. Did me a lot of good.

As the rehearsals went on, Kathleen found the music suited her well and it was easy for her to identify herself with the part. Carl Ebert's coaching and help too were inspiring.

Ann Ayers became a close friend: and Kathleen took under her wing Zoë Vlachopoulos the Greek soprano—Amore—who spoke no English, and who had learnt from some of the men at Glyndebourne to say one sentence: 'Don't be vague. H'ask for 'aig.' The three spent many hours together in the lovely gardens at Glyndebourne.

When the opera was produced on the 19th June 1947 it was enthusiastically received by the audience and favourably by most of the critics.

Harry Vincent, who made a special journey to see Kathleen at Glyndebourne, went round to her dressing room before a performance. She seemed rather depressed and showed him a poor notice of a previous performance. Harry, in an attempt to cheer her up, said: 'Well, I wouldn't worry too much. Perhaps he was feeling liverish. It often makes a difference to critics if they are not feeling well.' 'No, Harry,' said Kathleen, 'there must have been some reason why he said what he did. I want you to notice very carefully tonight whether I make the mistakes which he says I do. That will be far more help than trying to gloss over it and cheer me up.'

At the end however, Kathleen was overwhelmed with tributes, one of the most precious being accompanied by this note from Mr. and Mrs. Christie: 'Kathleen darling! So many people will want to give you flowers—I thought the little box would always remind you of today and that no singer I've *ever* heard gives me such complete satisfaction as our own *Orfeo*! Bless you, my dear, and may the angels bless you with your own heart's desire now and always. Love and best wishes from John and Audrey.'

The 'little box' in tortoise-shell and silver was inscribed *Kathleeen Ferrier, Orfeo, Glyndebourne June 19th, 1947, from John and Audrey.*

From Sir Steuart Wilson, then Music Director of the Arts Council of Great Britain, came this letter which was treasured:

Dear Miss Ferrier,

I came down on Tuesday to *Orfeo*. Of course I cannot agree with everything—but then, no one would expect admirers of *Orfeo* to be satisfied with anything except the imaginary production that we all have in our armchair reveries. The Elysian fields are Elysian because no one has ever seen them and we only imagine them, but your *Orfeo* is the nearest thing to the armchair dream that most of us will ever see.

The music is my 'Desert Island' choice. If I never heard anything else in my life I should choose the whole Opera. If I were limited to twenty minutes' music I would prefer the Hades and Elysian Fields and *Che puro ciel*.

I am not the sort of old opera goer who can say I heard X, Y and Z. I can only say that I have known the music for approximately forty-seven years and that it is lucky that during my lifetime I have heard it, at any rate in some particulars, as near my dreams as I could ever want.

Yours sincerely,
Steuart Wilson,
Music Director.

When the season at Glyndebourne ended, Kathleen and Win went on holiday in Devon, spending a quiet fortnight, walking and bathing, playing innumerable games of bar billiards and going early to bed. More than anything Kathleen needed relaxation, rest from the effort of talking to people, relief from the strain of performing. But even so, the score of *Das Lied von der Erde* was never far from her and she worked at it quietly every day.

By the 11th August when they returned to London she was full of health and vigour and ready for what lay before her—preparation for the first Edinburgh Festival.

When Bruno Walter went to the Frognal flat to rehearse and was introduced to Kathleen's father he said, 'You must be very proud of your daughter. She is a wonderful singer and fast making an international reputation. Soon she will be world famous.' 'Yes,' said her father, 'Kath's not doing badly.'

The period of rehearsal was one of great emotional tension for Kathleen. In childhood she had unconsciously acquired enough self control to shield her sensitiveness, but her unbounded admiration, affection and respect for Bruno Walter and her response to the sadness of Mahler's music sometimes broke through her defences. As Bruno Walter wrote later:

> We always had to interrupt the last part of the *Farewell*—she could not continue because her emotions overwhelmed her. Tears streamed down her cheeks; with all her will power and vigour she could not help it, and only by and by did she learn to control her feelings. But nothing could be further from her than sentimentality—in those tears spoke strength of feeling, not weakness, and a deep comprehension of another great heart.

Kathleen's first appearance at the Edinburgh Festival was at a chamber concert with Dr. Jacques and his orchestra. She sang *Prepare Thyself Zion* from the *Christmas Oratorio* and *Schlage doch gewünschte Stunde*. This concert prepared her in some measure for the ordeal to follow—the two performances of *Das Lied von der Erde*.

At the rehearsal Bruno Walter and the Vienna Philharmonic Orchestra met for the first time for many years—years in which some of the members of the orchestra had fallen victims of the Nazis. The awareness of the beauty of the music seemed

heightened by thoughts of Bruno Walter's association with the
Vienna of pre-war days. In this emotional setting it is not sur-
prising that conductor, orchestra and singers poignantly conveyed
Mahler's agonised farewell to life.

Both performances were well received by the audience,
although at that time Mahler's work was neither so well known
nor so popular as it is today. The critics' reactions were mixed:
all united in their admiration for Bruno Walter's conception,
but differing in their response to Mahler's music. *The Times*
carried the following:

> Mahler's symphonic song-cycle is a long work and intentionally
> a sad one. In effect it is the composer's leavetaking from the world.
> Here nostalgia is in place and though it may surfeit the hearer with
> excess of emotion and with its lush waves of rich orchestral sound,
> such a performance as Dr. Walter gave compels admiring surrender
> to the fascination of Mahler's resourcefulness.
>
> The performance was enhanced by the splendid singing of Miss
> Kathleen Ferrier, whose voice seemed to have gained an added
> richness and a power which surmounted the orchestral climaxes
> with ease. Her command of vocal colour to give dramatic ex-
> pressiveness to the words proved fully equal to the considerable
> demand of the songs, and these effects were accomplished without
> detriment to the beautiful quality of her tone.

Of the first Edinburgh Festival Kathleen wrote:

> It was unforgettable. The sun shone, the station was decked
> with flags, the streets were gay. Plays and ballet by the finest artists
> were being performed, literally morning, noon and night, and
> hospitality was showered upon guests and visitors by the so-called
> 'dour' Scots! What a mis-nomer!
>
> It was all so different from previous experiences of concerts.
> My daily routine had been mostly the same so far—travelling
> during the morning, rehearsing in the afternoon, performing at
> night, usually on an unchanging diet of sandwiches, and catching
> an early train next morning either home or to another engagement.
> To be able to unpack for a week and come to a concert fresh and
> thoroughly rehearsed was novel and delightful.

That was her way of putting it, but she could with truth
have said more. The Edinburgh Festival marked the beginning

of her work and friendship with Bruno Walter; her voice had developed 'an added richness and power'; she had resulting engagements both in Europe and America; she had now established her right to rank with artists of international standing.

CHAPTER TEN

Boat Train

'IN three months' time', said Kathleen on returning home from the Edinburgh Festival of 1947, 'I shall be singing *Das Lied von der Erde* in New York! Phantastisch! But in the meanwhile there are one or two little jobs to be attended to.'

The 'little jobs' included, taking part in performances of Elgar's *The Music Makers,* Mahler's *Kindertotenlieder* and *Third Symphony,* Beethoven's *Ninth Symphony,* Bach's *Mass in B Minor* and recording Brahms's *Alto Rhapsody.* There were also recitals, some of them broadcast, in which she sang folk songs, German Lieder and songs by classical and present-day composers. *The Rape of Lucretia* was revived, being produced in Newcastle, Bournemouth, Oxford and London. This London production gave Kathleen her first chance to sing at Covent Garden.

Still incredulous and sometimes overawed at the way her life was shaping, she summed it up:

'From Carlisle to Covent Garden in five years! Lucky Kath!'

On the first day of the New Year 1948 Mrs. Tillett, Mr. and Mrs. Roy Henderson and Miss Joan Cross were amongst the party of friends gathered on the platform at Waterloo to see Kathleen, accompanied by Mr. Tillett, off to America. A remark—'This will be the first of many long journeys'—expressed their common thoughts and wishes, as they watched the boat train disappear from sight.

Kathleen wrote so many letters that much of the story of this first short tour of North America can be told in her own words:

Cunard White Star,
R.M.S. *Mauretania*   Tuesday 6th January 1948.
Dearest Win,

Hello, love! Here I am, propped up in bed, having a gorgeous breakfast and feeling the complete diva.

Heavens, I never expected to enjoy this trip so much. We've had sunshine, gales and heavy swells and I've never turned a hair —even when I have seen other folk in distress!

I don't know where to start, but our main conversation is food! I have never ever seen such dishes and we are being spoiled by the chief steward who thinks up meals for us, so that we start with tomato juice, caviar with all the trimmings, soup, fish, lobster or salmon, beef steaks, joints of all descriptions, and the most amazing sweets ever. Baked ice-cream—that is ice-cream on cake with meringue all round it, or ice-cream with cherries in brandy, and the brandy lit with a match till there are blue flames all over it. Oh dear, I keep thinking about your struggling along to make the joint spin out, but I'll send some parcels when I arrive—then you can both have a tuck in.

Arrived in New York, she wrote:

What a city—it is just a fairyland of good things and wonderful buildings, and all the time I am wishing you could both be here to share these excitements and pleasures.

The voyage was wonderful and sheer luxury and I felt very prima donna when I was interviewed on the boat on arrival and pictures taken of me leaning over the starboard side!

I've had flowers from Hans Schneider and a lovely plant from Ruth Draper.

It is all a wonderful experience, but home will be lovely too. I just hope all is well with you both and that you are getting plenty to eat. Think of me on the 15th and keep your fingers crossed—it's going to be a terrific strain but reckon I'll survive somehow!—shall be with you on the 9th Feb. at the latest. Whoopee!

A few days later:

All is well here except I've got a runny cold. The rooms are so hot and the streets so icy, the change of atmosphere has been too much to cope with. Yesterday, I had no voice at all, but today, my nose is running like a tap, so all is well—it'll soon be right now!

I have had two rehearsals with Bruno Walter and he is very pleased but I keep my fingers crossed all the time. There seems to be a lot of publicity about this concert and Alma Mahler (Mahler's wife) is going to be there—my photie was in the *New York Times* yesterday.

Did I tell you Ruth Draper sent me a lovely azalea (bright red).

If my cold is better tomorrow, I'm having dinner with her—what a thrill!

I'm in the throes of signing a contract for next year, but as there seems to be more paying out than receiving, I'm not thrilled—but expect it will work out all right. Look after yourselves, loves. Will write again and let you know what the results of the concert are.

Friday 16th January 1948.

Dearest Win,

Just a short scribble. I know you'll be wondering how I got on. Well, Bruno Walter was thrilled—I've never known him to open out so—he said I was making musical history (honest)!

Some of the critics are enthusiastic, others unimpressed. I'll quote from some—

New York Telegram.—Miss F. ought to make a permanent addition to the whole wing of New York music. The voice is warm and vibrant, easily produced and capable of rich application of colour. Phrasing and diction both showed a sure grip of style and content.

N.Y. Sun.—The high hopes held for K.F., the English mezzo, (!) were not fulfilled. Miss F. has a clear, clean and clinging voice and she is a musicianly artist. But her voice has neither the breadth nor depth to convey all of what Mahler meant and she sounded to be more *soprano* than mezzo. One did not feel either the poise or the authority for so heavy a burden. Her uncertain pronunciation of the German text was also disturbing.

New York Times.—Miss F. had but recently emerged from a bad cold. Her voice became freer as she went on. She could not, however, give full significance to her text and music. Some time before the end was reached, *Das Lied* was becoming langweilig, lachrymose, old-fashioned.

I've shown you the two bad ones. There are two more ecstatic ones in the *N.Y. Tribune* and something else. It is very disappointing. I had been in bed three days with the worst cold I've ever had, but I had Ruth Draper's doctor and he worked miracles—he douched my nose and painted my throat, and quite honestly, what with all the good food and rest, I have, myself, never felt in such good trim. My soft top notes came as I have never known them—I was a bit nervous but did it all from memory except for a few words which I hid behind my programme, and Bruno Walter told me today that my German was pure and classic and he's thrilled, so

I don't really mind—only I wanted to come home sort of top of the class!

This afternoon the performance was even better—I thought the tenor was excellent, but he's hardly had a kind word! Mr. Tillett said someone next to him said, 'What a small voice' (the place holds 3,500). But if they knew the score they would realise that I have to start *pp* and stay there more or less until the orchestra gets noisy.

The American agents have rung up, wanting me to do a recital in New York whilst I'm here, but I'm not going to until I've done some Lieder with Bruno Walter! YES!—he's going to give me some lessons when I get back from Chicago—*what* an opportunity!

He is truly thrilled with me and my German and interpretation, and is already seeing to my dates for next year, so I don't mind so much now.

I suppose it's good for one not to hit the headlines all the time, but I did want to on this occasion.

Well love, that's about all. It hasn't ended in a blaze of glory, but it's all experience.

Loads of love,
Not so Klever Kaff.

Her disappointment was mitigated by this extract from a letter by Leopold Stokowski to the manager of the New York Philharmonic Society:

> The mezzo-soprano who sang in Mahler's *Das Lied von der Erde* yesterday was simply superb. Her voice was so full and beautiful, the intonation always perfect, the phrasing so elastic, the interpretation so eloquent. Altogether it was a superb performance and I wish to thank you for the pleasure I had in listening to it and to congratulate you on having chosen such a perfect artist for this masterpiece.

After these two performances in the Carnegie Hall came concerts in Ottawa and Chicago.

The following letter was written before her second concert in Chicago:

23rd January 1948.

Dearest Win,

I wonder where I left you! We travelled from New York on Monday last and were given roomettes on the train—all right, but frightfully draughty! I slept in everything I had, including my new woollie breeks, but I didn't sleep much, though the trains are very smooth, the beds are sprung so. I bounced up and down all night like a rubber ball.

Well, we arrived in Chicago, had breakfast on the station and caught train immediately for Ottawa—two hours away. I slept most of the way, I was terrified of the concert, but there were about 900 there, and there wasn't a whisper, and they were thrilled to bits. Wasn't that good?

The next day we came to Chicago to this sumpschuss Hotel— I'll never be able to pay my bill! I was met by four women reporters and three photographers and thoroughly enjoyed myself.

That concert went well too, though it was in a cinema and very dead and I had spotlights and couldn't see a thing, but as you can see from the cutting, I can't have been so bad. Cassidy is the most notable critic outside N.Y.—for all the Middle West—so I'm pleased. I didn't know she was there and finished off with the *Stuttering Lovers* and had them all in fits, so perhaps that put her in a good humour!

My big recital is tonight in this hotel in the ballroom—it's snowing horizontally across my window—I shall be staying in and catching up on letters.

This is the loveliest city ever—walked along the shores of Lake Michigan yesterday—all frozen and stretching as far as eye could see. It was seven degrees below zero last night!! Loving every minute now!

Chicago Daily Tribune—23rd January 1948.

WHEN LEHMANN AND FERRIER SING THE SAME NIGHT
A TRIP TO PARK RIDGE SOLVES THE PROBLEM

By Claudia Cassidy

Not much in this world of theater and music could keep me from Orchestra Hall tonight, when Lotte Lehmann sings Schubert, but it is nice to know I will suffer no twinge of distress at missing Kathleen Ferrier's Chicago debut in the Blackstone Hotel, because I heard Miss Ferrier in Park Ridge Wednesday night, thru the courtesy of the Maine Township Community Concert Association. She was worth the trip too.

Where Mme. Lehmann is the supreme revelation of the art of song, Miss Ferrier is a notable newcomer with the germ of greatness. A tall girl with blonder hair than her pictures suggest, she looks more Irish than English, particularly when she spins Irish folklore with a touch of gossamer mischief. But that is a sidelight. Her essential quality is a kind of bedrock simplicity, a native serenity stemming from strength, and her great gift is a singularly beautiful contralto, almost as natural as Flagstad's soprano in placement and unmistakably her own in its firm, dark texture and supple yet satisfyingly solid tone. Her range just now seems a bit skimpy at the top, but she is too wise to do any forcing. Let it come—with that wonderful middle voice and that velvet-slipping-downstairs of her descending scale, she can wait.

With Arpad Sandor competently at the piano, Miss Ferrier sang a full-scale program in the big style. Handel, including the noble *Largo*. Gluck, to give us rewarding glimpses of her Glyndebourne *Orfeo*. Schubert—well, Schubert is elusive. *Gretchen am Spinnrade* was valid music drama, beautifully done, but *Erlkoenig*, which can be all things to all singers, tried too hard and overshot the mark. The English group was quite lovely—Vaughan Williams's *Silent Noon*, Stanford's silvery song called *The Fairy Lough*, Britten's way with the *Salley Gardens* and Hughes's *I have a Bonnet*, and the delectable tale of *The Spanish Lady*. But most extraordinary of all were Brahms's *Four Serious Songs* which she sang with courage, not in mourning. She did not make them problem songs, so no one was baffled by them. They were sombre but not sodden and I have rarely found them so moving. *O Death how Bitter* which is magnificent in itself, was superbly sung.

*   *   *

As he had promised, Bruno Walter gave Kathleen some lessons on Lieder when she returned to New York, lessons which were an inspiration to her and a revelation of the wealth of music which she had just begun to explore. Thrilled by the help and advice that he had given her, and assured that they would work together again as soon as their engagements permitted, Kathleen boarded the *Queen Mary* and sailed for home.

New realms were indeed opened by her work with Bruno Walter: a wealth of lovely music in the Lieder which she studied with him, a depth of interpretation which grew under his influence, an intuitive grasp of a world of emotional experience quite foreign, on the face of it, to her own temperament, yet striking some chords in her deepest being to which she could not but respond—the world of Mahler.

Summing up her six months of music from September 1947 to February 1948, Kathleen wrote:

As a result of my being heard by Professor Bruno Walter, this season was to prove the most exciting that I have known so far.

After a holiday in Devonshire, where I had memorised the work I had to sing for the now famous first Edinburgh Festival (*Das Lied von der Erde*—Gustav Mahler), I arrived home again in Hampstead.

In the midst of my unpacking, the telephone rang, and to my amazement it was Professor Walter who had flown from America the previous day and who, without waiting to catch up with lost sleep, was proposing to come up to my flat to start rehearsals! I was alarmed at the thought of the steps he would have to climb— he is now seventy-two years old—and even more alarmed at his possible reactions to my piano which is an upright, one which I won in a piano-playing competition when I was sixteen and now no longer all that might be desired! I felt sure that my memorised German words which I had learned so painfully would desert me, but a taxi from the West End to Hampstead does not take long enough to allow of too many anxious thoughts, and I was greeting the great man on the doorstep almost before I had found my score in the chaos of my unpacking.

After this first rehearsal, Peter Pears, the tenor soloist, and I had about fifteen hours intensive study with piano of this particular work with Professor Walter. It was quite memorable to me. Professor Walter had been friend, student and confidant of Mahler, and he lived and loved every note of the score, playing and conducting the whole work from memory. My greatest difficulty was to restrain my sobs in the last heartbreaking 'Abschied', and at the second rehearsal I was unsuccessful and held up work for about half-an-hour while I blew my nose, mopped my streaming eyes and tried to apologise for being a nuisance, all at one time! The intensity of this work and the emotion of Professor Walter had caught me unawares, but I was patted on the back and told, 'It's all right, my child, they all do.' But at all piano and, later, orchestral rehearsals I could never sing the last song without a lump in my throat and it was only at the first performance in Edinburgh I felt I could enjoy it and now make others weep instead of myself! I had not suffered so much since playing the part of *Orfeo* at Glyndebourne Opera the previous spring, when I lost my beautiful *Euridice* after defying Hades and Elysium for her!

On 1st January 1948 I sailed with my manager to New York to repeat the Edinburgh performance of *Das Lied von der Erde* with Bruno Walter, but this time with the New York Philharmonic, instead of the Vienna Philharmonic Orchestra, in Carnegie Hall on three different dates. This was something I had never believed possible in my wildest dreams and I was excited, to say the least of it! I had had one day to pack, having been singing to the last moment, but it was encouraging to think that I shouldn't need coupons for anything I had left behind!

Our journey seemed as though it might never start, for, when we arrived at Southampton there was a stevedores' strike: eventually, however, we were gliding away from Southampton, and every minute of the next five days was an experience and a delight. The ship was the *Mauretania*, newly painted and decorated after her war service and a joy to behold and inhabit. I will not make mouths water by my description of the food and the comfort, but it was overwhelming after eight years of austerity.

The first sight of New York has to be seen to be believed, and with snow, sunshine and high blue, clear sky, it was more than impressive. We were through the customs and in a cab in record time, despite several photographers and newspaper men all asking questions and taking photographs at the same time. Our hotel was very central, exceedingly comfortable and unbearably hot. The first persons we saw were Mr. and Mrs. Benno Moisewitsch, who were also making it a home for a little while, so there were rejoicings all round and much chatter! From then on, every minute was occupied—shop gazing—museum visiting—meeting the American manager—seeing Broadway illuminated by a million lights—rehearsing with pianist for some recitals I had to do in and about Chicago—more piano rehearsals with Bruno Walter— and coping with the well-known American hospitality! Ruth Draper, whom I had met only once in London, welcomed me with flowers, invited me to dinner and tea, left a box at my disposal for myself and friends at the theatre where she was playing, and generally spoiled me like an only child!

As my first concert at Carnegie Hall drew near, I ceased all merry-making and concentrated only on rehearsals, not talking too much and going to bed early. I had developed a cold, due to the extremes of temperature, and I was being careful. If I were indisposed and couldn't sing, I should not be able to pay my hotel bill—a frightening thought. But all was well and the three perfor-

mances were given without a hitch—and included in the applause
were asides from the orchestra, such as 'Bravo Beautiful'—very
American, but balm to a singer's soul, when such praise comes
sincerely from an instrumental player!

The last performance was broadcast all over America and the
manager of the orchestra told me that there were between fifteen
and twenty million listeners! One letter, as a result of this relay,
came from the famous conductor, Stokowski, and was a glowing
tribute—one which I treasure highly.

Immediately after this last concert, my accompanist, manager
and I caught one of the famous diesel trains to Chicago. They are
very quiet and comfortable and I think the dinner we had on this
train surpassed any meal I had ever had, it was wonderful—and
served by negro waiters with ear to ear grins of shining white
teeth. My accompanist would whisper to a waiter that I was
English and therefore starved, also a singer who needed fattening
up, and there would appear more butter than even I could manage!!
He was a great tease, but a terrific help on our travels and in the
delicate matter of tipping, saved us much thought and embarrassment.

I was a little worried about my first recital concert—I had made
up a programme of Handel, Gluck in Italian, Schubert in German,
the Brahms *Serious Songs* and English folk songs. My first concert
was at Ottawa, about two hours away from Chicago, and I had
travelled from 4.30 p.m. the previous day, and not having slept
very much, was feeling a little jaded by the time we arrived—about
noon. The town looked small and the houses were mostly wooden,
and I wondered where our audience would come from, and Oh
dear! *why* had I put down the Brahms *Serious Songs*? I dressed for
the concert, feeling slightly sick, and was taken down to the hall.
My manager, who had no rouge to hide his pallor, was looking as
I felt, and even my voluble pianist was quiet.

The concert was in a lovely school hall, holding about a thousand
people and it was crammed full! I never knew where they all came
from, but from the first to the last notes of the piano there was a
breathless silence, and then such an ovation after my first group
as to dispel all doubts as to the suitability of the programme.

After the first concert the next three recitals went well and in
each case the hall was filled to capacity. One of the things I remember
learning at school was the names of the great lakes, and I had to
pinch myself to realise I could look out of my room window in

Chicago immediately on to Lake Michigan stretching—cold and frozen—as far as the eye could see!

And now back to New York again for a week's holiday before boarding the *Queen Mary* on February 4th. There were no concerts looming in the near future to worry me. I had the money to pay my hotel bill—I could relax or hustle as the mood took me. The bracing cold of New York seemed to produce energy in me, and I went from one excitement to another. Lunches and dinners with Mr. and Mrs. Schnabel, with Bruno Walter and his daughter, with Elisabeth Schumann, with Ruth Draper and many American friends—shopping with endless window gazing—days in the Metropolitan and Frick Museums—a visit to the 76th floor of the Empire State Building to pay my income tax (!) and many memorable hours of enjoyment.

The journey home was uneventful, though the ship 'dipped her elbows in the sea' all the way, due to a 'confused swell'! The glasses and cutlery chased each other across the tables in the dining room, and we had to pour water on the table cloths to make them a little less mobile. We were several hours late arriving at Southampton and I was home by 5.30 p.m. on the 10th February —only just in time for a performance of *The Dream of Gerontius* at the Albert Hall the next day.

AT SILLOTH

KATHLEEN FERRIER
Contralto

A new singer of remarkable talent.
Manchester Guardian

MANCHESTER TUESDAY CONCERTS

Miss Kathleen Ferrier, a new singer of remarkable talent, was heard yesterday in the Houldsworth Hall, Manchester. A full, rich contralto voice, flexible throughout its compass and capable of lovely shades of tone and expression, is rare in these days, and as the possessor of such a voice Miss Ferrier is far better equipped by nature than are many contraltos who enjoy considerable fame. And she sings with feeling and intelligence, using her vocal gifts as the servant of her temperament.

G.A.H.—*Manchester Guardian*

LIVERPOOL PHILHARMONIC HALL

Whoever induced Kathleen Ferrier to sing at the concert given by Leslie Bridgewater and his salon orchestra on Saturday evening has my gratitude. She is a great contralto, and one worthy to be mentioned as a possible successor to Clara Butt. It is a long time since we heard anyone sing Handel's " Where'er you walk" with such telling simplicity and dignity. It was just plain, honest singing without any frills, but with the effortless charm of the artist. She has range and quality of tone.

Liverpool Evening Express

ORATORIO AND MISCELLANEOUS

The Messiah Performance was enriched by a beautiful rendering of the contralto part by Kathleen Ferrier. Her voice had a lovely creamy quality. The air " He shall feed His Flock" glowed with tender conviction. The significance of " He was Despised " was deepened by beauty and sincerity of expression.

Evening Chronicle, St. Annes-on-Sea

" ELIJAH "

Miss Kathleen Ferrier sang with great charm and sincerity. She was good in the dramatic part of the Queen when singing with the chorus, in the solo " Woe unto them," and in the aria " O rest in the Lord." This was rendered with great sympathy and expression. Miss Ferrier has one of the purest contralto voices, and she left the impression that she will be one of the country's leading oratorio singers in the near future.

Runcorn Weekly News

Miss Kathleen Ferrier, who has a very beautiful contralto voice, sang Brahms and modern British songs with considerable finish and imagination.

Liverpool Daily Post

EXTRACTS FROM PRESS NOTICES
Quoted in the leaflet

KATHLEEN IN 1944

GLYNDEBOURNE, 1946

With Ernest Ansermet (centre) and members of the company

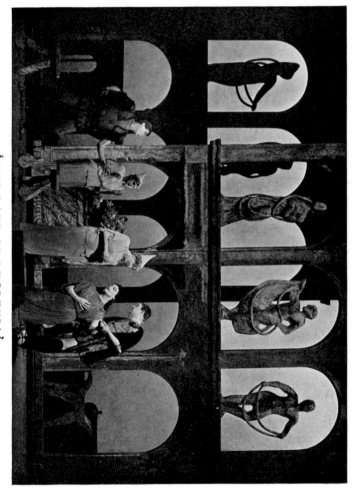

'THE RAPE OF LUCRETIA'

The Suicide Scene

DEVON HOLIDAY WITH WIN, 1946

ANOTHER HOLIDAY PICTURE

CHAPTER ELEVEN

K. K.

The laundryman missed a call at the Frognal flat; the only course was for Kathleen and Win to tackle the growing pile of linen. In steamy atmosphere, turning the table wringer at great speed, Kathleen said: 'If only my public could see me now!'

There were several points in this remark: a contrast between the homeliness of the kitchen and the glamour of the concert platform; a friendly dig at some of the artificialities associated with musical performances; a quiet feeling that no matter if the public *could* see her—she had nothing to lose thereby. For now she was on top of the world, vigorous, gay and at once confident in her supreme ability and humble in face of her master —music.

It is right, therefore, in telling the story of her life to pause, and forsaking chronology, to keep, as it were open house for a time at Frognal, so that friends may call and in some measure see what she was like personally during the years that she was making her major contribution to music.

So far Win had managed to run the household with occasional help from Kathleen when she was home and with the willing assistance of 'our father'. A woman came in two or three times a week; but now it became obvious that changes must be made. Kathleen needed someone to see to her clothes and her correspondence, 'our father', though lively and interested as ever, was eighty years old, and twice in the course of a week had fallen asleep with a cigarette in his mouth, burning a hole in his jacket sleeve. It was becoming unsafe for him to be alone all day. Win, who was now the head of a school in Chiswick, was finding the housekeeping and the travelling too much in addition to her work. The problem was to find a suitable person to take over. Roy Henderson eventually came to the rescue by suggesting a pupil of his, Patricia Jewett, who needed somewhere to live and who was willing to do the housekeeping while studying singing. This arrangement worked well and Paddy became one of the family. After this, entertaining was a little easier, but Kathleen, anxious not to give Paddy too much work, often took people to a restaurant.

Although she enjoyed going occasionally to the Ritz for lunch, to the Savoy for dinner and dancing, her favourite restaurant was Casa Prada in the Euston Road, to which Parry Jones had taken her. The proprietor, his son and daughter, took a warm, personal interest in their customers and there was a welcoming family atmosphere which appealed very much to Kathleen. The food was interesting, well cooked, and the wine good. On the walls hung autographs, embroidered on linen and framed, of famous people who had patronised the restaurant. When Kathleen was asked to sign her name so that it could be added to the collection, she was delighted. 'Recognition at last!' she said, joking, but flattered by the request. This autograph still hangs on the wall.

When working in London Kathleen often went to Casa Prada after a morning rehearsal. If the concert was to take place the same evening she needed a good lunch because her next meal would be after the performance. In the afternoon she would often sleep for several hours and then, before dressing for the concert would have a cup of tea and a boiled egg. She often took with her a bottle of orange juice in case her throat became dry, for although she enjoyed a 'corpse reviver', she never drank alcohol before a concert.

When the concert was over she looked forward to a drink and perhaps one or two puffs at a cigarette. Before her professional career began she had smoked quite a lot, but now she limited herself strictly to an occasional cigarette when a concert was not imminent. After the performance was over she was excited and strung up and this was the time when a leisurely meal with a few congenial people was really enjoyable. Then indeed she felt able to relax and to laugh and talk as much as she liked. This was only permissible, in her opinion, if there was no concert the following day. She resisted sternly the temptation to lead too social a life: after what she considered a period of 'gadding about', she wrote in her diary, 'Going out too much. This must stop!'

Although she was doing much work and her fees steadily rising, she did not yet feel financially secure enough to spend money extravagantly. Realising that illness or accident might rob her of her voice and livelihood she made what provision was possible. She insured herself against loss of earnings through illness and put away some money in National Savings and Defence Bonds.

Early in 1949 she mentioned casually to Win that she had been to the doctor for an examination. Gradually the story came out. At one time she had received a sharp blow from someone's elbow on the side of her breast. This had worried her because it had been a widely held belief in her girlhood that blows such as this caused cancer. Although she forgot about it for months on end, every now and then there would be a slight sensation in her breast and down her arm which reminded her of the incident. Although she tried to persuade herself that it was all imagination, the worry persisted. Even as long ago as 1942, when the decision to move to London had been taken, she had thought that if eventually she had to have an operation, it would be an advantage to be near the London hospitals. In 1944 she had mentioned her worry to 'Prof' and he had insisted on her having an examination. He had taken her to a doctor and waited for the verdict. It was satisfactory—no sign of a lump or of any-thing wrong—a reassuring confirmation. 'I thought it was only sense to have it', she said rather apologetically, 'instead of going on worrying over nothing. Now I can put it out of my mind'.

The subject was not mentioned again and indeed she appeared strong and vigorous: it seemed impossible that anything could be wrong. She played golf whenever it could be fitted in. She went for long walks on Hampstead Heath and when away on tour walked as much as possible. Always on holiday she enjoyed wandering for miles over the countryside.

She sought permission from the landlord to use a small piece of ground behind the flats and began to make a garden. The site was unpromising: it was on a level with the top of the coal sheds; it had to be reached by climbing a short ladder; it was over-shadowed by a large poplar tree; and it was overrun by cats. Kathleen however began reading gardening books, buying seeds and plants and gradually turned it into a pretty little garden. In this she was enthusiastically aided by Paddy, who had worked in a market garden during the war and missed the open-air life.

Kathleen also turned her attention to the flat and made im-provements. Having learnt from Mrs. Tillett, 'Prof' and other friends whose homes she visited, to appreciate good furniture, she began to buy a little; a Chippendale table, a small chest of drawers. She started almost from scratch and slowly, as time and money allowed, replaced the existing furniture by things more to her liking, more in accordance with her developing tastes. From the Maitlands, whose collection of paintings included Degas, van Gogh, Gauguin and others, she learnt a good deal about pictures. She visited picture galleries with them in London and Edinburgh and later in Holland and Italy. It was they who gave her Winston Churchill's book *Painting as a Pastime,* which encouraged her to begin to paint.

Now that there was not so much *learning* of music to be done, Kathleen managed to find a little more time for reading. For light relief she read *Clochemerle* by Chevallier and *Our hearts were Young and Gay,* by Cornelia Otis Skinner. After her American tours and in the light of some of her experiences in the smaller towns in America, she was very much amused by *It Gives Me Great Pleasure,* by Emily Kimborough. Two books by Marjorie Kinnan Rawlings were favourites—*Cross Creek* and *The Yearling.* Much of her reading, however, was connected with music. As well as Elisabeth Schumann's book on *German Song,* Lotte Lehman's *More than Singing* and Harry Plunket Greene's *Interpretation in Song,* she read *J. S. Bach,* by Albert Schweitzer, the lives of Schubert and Schumann in the Master Musicians Series, and *Brahms,* by Ralph Hill. *My Life,* by Isadora Duncan, also interested her very much, and after meeting Bruno Walter she read his autobiography, *Theme and Variations* and *Memoirs and Letters* by Alma Mahler.

One book, *Of Lena Geyer*, by Marcia Davenport, made a great impression on her. It was the story of an American opera singer, who at one point had to choose between a love affair and her career. '"I shall try to be yours and live for my art, too", said Lena to her lover, "but I must be fair to you. If I cannot do both, you know what my choice will have to be!"' Later she said, '"It cannot be done, I would only ruin myself and torture you by trying to do it. I am not the great love, dear Louis—for anybody. I cannot be, I am only"—she made a futile gesture—"a throat".'

Although Kathleen never said in so many words that she felt that this applied to herself, she talked a good deal about the book and said how true to life it was. She had fallen in love with a delightful man. They had been very happy together and for some time she had envisaged the possibility of marrying him. Part of her yearned for a homely family life, for children and for someone to care for and protect her. At times she questioned whether her career merited all the striving and sacrifice that it entailed. 'Mother, is it worth it!' she exclaimed on one occasion when she saw the people streaming into the Albert Hall to hear her. Had the man she loved been a professional musician it would perhaps have been possible to reach some compromise. But although he enjoyed listening to music, he could not enter into what took up the major part of her life and thought. As time went on it was borne in upon her that marriage with him would be a mistake. Realising that the claims of a husband would conflict with her singing career, she made her decision. At the time she said very little about it. In a letter to Win, a remark that 'I've decided that I am fated to be a lone she-wolf' was the only indication that the choice had been made. Into her singing of the *Frauenliebe und Leben* she poured her longing and regret.

One can understand how at this time she dreaded singing *Du bist die Ruh*, for fear of bursting into tears.

> ' Thou art my rest, my joy untold
> The secret that my longings hold
> To thee, in joy and suffering great
> My heart and eyes I consecrate.'

It was a particular joy to Kathleen, but joy tinged with envy, to be with those of her friends who were happily married. 'Isn't it lovely', she said, 'to see a couple so well matched as Gerald and Enid? They can work together and when he is writing a book she types it for him.' And to Ena Mitchell she said, 'Marriage is not for me, but I have it in my heart to envy you and Bill.'

While on her way to Carlisle by train, Kathleen shared her sandwiches with a woman in the compartment who seemed distressed. It transpired that she had been to hospital to see her husband, whose leg had been amputated. 'Never mind, love,' said Kathleen, 'you've got *him*, and he's still got two arms to put round you.'

Kathleen had a great store of affection which flowed out to people. Accepting them as she did at their face value, without reservation or criticism, she made friends wherever she went. Yet she remembered, when they turned up at her concerts, those whom she had not met for years. Girls and teachers connected with her school-days, telephonists who had worked with her in the Post Office, all were greeted with joy *and* by name when they went to see her in the artists' room.

On one occasion her Silloth friends, Bill and Eleanor Coyd, Frances and Tony Bragg, made a long difficult journey through the snow to attend one of her concerts. Afterwards they went round to the artists' room which was seething with people. They edged their way towards the spot where Kathleen was standing signing autographs—all except Bill, who stood quietly by the door. Having greeted the others, she suddenly caught sight of him. Making her way through the crowd, she flung her arms round him.

For children Kathleen had a special tenderness. When she visited Win's Infant School she was much amused to see the children playing at houses and shops, washing and baking and doing woodwork. But when they sang for her and played the percussion band, she had to turn away her head to hide her tears. In telling her friend about it later she said, 'You *must* see them, Ena. They're lovely! I sat in the bus afterwards and cried all the way to Baker Street at the thought of their innocent little flower faces.'

Kathleen was not interested in science. Politics were anathema —partly because of her hatred of arguments and disagreements. Although indignant when she came across examples of injustice or racial prejudice—as when a learned Negro professor had difficulty in gaining admittance to one of her concerts in America —yet her interest had a humanitarian rather than a political basis. Much of the music which most inspired her was religious, yet she seldom, if ever, discussed religion and had no ties with any particular church.

This is in some measure the person you would have met, when you called at Frognal. And as you left and went down the steps and down the hill you might have reflected that, despite the easy friendliness, the simplicity and candour, there were hints also of spiritual remoteness, even of sublimity: but they were the barest hints; for only in song did she express her intensity and range of emotion, her sincerity of purpose, her spirituality.

CHAPTER TWELVE

New Worlds

AFTER the production of *The Rape of Lucretia* in Holland in 1946, Peter Diamand, the Dutch impresario, had tried to arrange a concert tour, but it was not until April, 1948, that Kathleen was able to undertake her first engagements there as a solo artist.

As well as a broadcast of *Kindertotenlieder* from Hilversum, several recitals had been arranged. The first one took place in British House, Amsterdam. On the day when the booking opened, Miss Schill, the British Council agent in Holland, noticed that a queue had formed early at the box office. Thinking that Kathleen was comparatively unknown in Holland at that time, she was surprised and enquired the reason. Apparently people had heard her on the radio and were anxious to get tickets. By lunch time all were sold, and this happened for the following three concerts.

The following programme is typical of those given in Holland at this time.

PROGRAMME

Nederlandsch Impressariaat Heerengracht 478 Amsterdam. Tel. 34937.

Concertgebouw (kl. saal)   Zondag 2 Mei 1948—8.15 uur
Liederenavond

KATHLEEN FERRIER

Aan de vleugel: *Isja Rossican.*
Programma:

1.	(a)	Prepare thyself Zion (Weinachts-Oratorium)	J. S. Bach (1685–1750)

(b)	Like as the lovelorn Turtle (Atalanta)	G. F. Handel (1685–1759)
(c)	Come to me soothing sleep	
(d)	Pack clouds away	
2. (a)	Die Junge Nonne	Franz Schubert (1797–1828)
(b)	Erster Verlust	
(c)	Gretchen am Sprinnrade	
(d)	Erlkönig	

Pauze

3. (a)	Liebestreu	Joh. Brahms (1838–1897)
(b)	Sapphische Ode	
(c)	Minnelied	
4. (a)	Silent Noon	Vaughan Williams (geb. 1872)
(b)	A Piper	Michael Head (geb. 1900)
(c)	Star Candles	Michael Head
(d)	Flower Song (Rape of Lucretia)	Benjamin Britten (geb. 1913)
(e)	Down by the Salley Gardens (Folk song)	bewerkt door B. Britten
(f)	Oliver Cromwell (Suffolk Nursery Rhyme)	bewerkt door B. Britten

Folk songs were sometimes included as well as *Rahoon* by Moeran and the *Three Psalms* by Edmund Rubbra.
She wrote from Amsterdam:

It's simply lovely here and I'm having such an easy time though an average of a concert every other day. Peter Diamand takes me everywhere by car and is so business-like and musical, it's a joy. He has been to every concert and broadcast.

The pianist is Russian-cum-Dutch and a poppet. We converse in pidgin German and original deaf and dumb and get on very well. I've had a real rest and feel I'm not singing so badly, and have ravishing notices. Last night I was at Rotterdam. I get bouquets at every performance—three at the Hague!—and am being ruined! Today some people are taking me to see the bulb fields, and from the few I saw in the train from the Hook, it should be a wonderful sight. Otokar Kraus turned up yesterday—he's doing some shows at the opera—so we're meeting for a good talk this morning.

I loved *Impresario* and couldn't stop reading until I'd finished it —now I'm reading *Huckleberry Finn*—Mark Twain—and finding it delicious.

The food is not so meaty as it was—I haven't *seen* a steak—but there is lots to eat—eggs and fish mainly, but all delicious. But I never get a salad anywhere like yours and Paddy's.

All clothes are on points so there's nothing to buy, but it *is* a pleasure to walk round Amsterdam with its canals and trees and lovely houses.

A press notice, 12th April 1948, written by Bertus van Lier in *Het Parool*, reads:

It is not surprising that the owner of this wonderful contralto voice became famous in so little time, and that Bruno Walter immediately gave her an engagement in America, after he had heard her in Edinburgh! For really: all that one can wish for in singing in one's dreams is here materialized: a voice like a bell, varying from velvety softness to silvery lustre, a technique so effortlessly perfect that everyone stops believing that singing is difficult; apart from the simplicity and purity of interpretation as one very seldom hears: in a word delightful.

We can but advise music lovers to go and hear her sing, on 22nd April, in the small hall at the Concertgebouw! She was excellently accompanied by pianist Isja Rossican.

A week after her return from Holland she was due to go there again to take part in a performance of *Das Lied von der Erde*, conducted by van Otterloo in Utrecht. So far she had managed to avoid flying but on this occasion there was no time to go by sea. A coloured postcard of the bulb fields arrived home:

Had a grand journey though my stomach dropped a yard when we took off! Had lunch served and magazines and sat back and pretended not to feel white about the gills!! Was in Amsterdam by noon—isn't it amazing! *Das Lied* went very well at Utrecht. Everybody seemed pleased. Had three bouquets—beginning to expect 'em!

After a recital in Amsterdam she flew home again, arriving at 4 p.m.—just in time to attend a recording session which lasted from 6 until 9 p.m.

Two months later Kathleen was back yet again to take part in the Holland Festival of 1948. In Amsterdam and Scheveningen she sang in performances of *Das Lied von der Erde,* conducted by George Szell. This was the end of her third visit to Holland in the space of four months.

After a short holiday in Northern Ireland and two months work in England, Kathleen was due to go by air to Scandinavia. Before setting off for Copenhagen she remarked that she hoped the pilot would not take his hands off the handlebars while they were over the North Sea. This was her first long flight, and although in time she became used to flying, she never completely lost her nervousness. She often amused her friends by telling of her first experience of the take-off. So absorbed was she in gripping the arms of her chair and mentally lifting the plane off the ground, that when the air hostess touched her shoulder she was so startled that she almost leapt to her feet.

In Copenhagen she stayed with the Hansen family before her concert on the 20th September. It was to be with the Royal Orchestra, conducted by Egisto Tango and as songs with orchestral accompaniment were required, her choice of programme was limited. She sang:

Bach: *Prepare thyself Zion* (*Christmas Oratorio*)
Byrd: *Cradle Song*
Gluck: *Che Faro* (*Orfeo*)
Handel: *Art Thou Troubled* (*Rodelinda*)
Purcell: *Hark, the ech'ing air.*

On Sunday, 26th September a Memorial Service for Count Bernadotte took place in the Swedish Church, and she was asked to sing *Schlage doch*—a very moving occasion.

After recitals in Copenhagen, Naested and Holbäck, she flew home.

Writing later, Einer Gylling the Danish impresario said: 'The first time Kathleen came here was in 1948, when she appeared with the Royal Orchestra as a soloist, and a few days later she gave her first recital in the Odd Fellow Palais, a concert which caused the most remarkable reviews I have ever seen. One of our critics wrote that 'one could not write a criticism after such a concert, one should rather ask a great poet to write a beautiful poem for Kathleen Ferrier.'

'Kathleen went to several provincial Music Clubs and they all still talk about the concert as being the best they have ever had.'

He added that Kathleen always called him 'Einer Kleiner'.

This visit to Denmark was the last trip abroad in 1948, the rest of the year being taken up with concerts in England and Scotland.

By the middle of January 1949 Kathleen was back in Holland once more for a series of recitals, taking Phyllis Spurr with her. This was a great comfort. They got on very well together, and rehearsals were never either so long or so difficult as with a previously unknown accompanist. Though they were used to working together, Kathleen insisted on rehearsal before each concert, and this even when they were giving the same programme several days in succession.

When she was on tour, nothing was allowed to interfere with her work. It would have been easy for her to spend much time and energy in going to parties, and indeed she sometimes had great difficulty in refusing invitations without giving offence. But she was obviously sincere, so people usually accepted her quietly firm refusal graciously.

Days were planned so that she and Phyllis were rested and fresh for each performance. Usually after having a light breakfast in bed they rehearsed intensively for about an hour and then went for a brisk walk before lunch. When they were travelling there was an arrangement that they would not talk at all except at mealtimes. If it were possible, they both had a rest in bed in the afternoon. Kathleen never ate much before a performance, and as the evening concerts finished late, it was sometimes well after midnight before she began her evening meal.

After four visits to Holland Kathleen was feeling very much at home there. The staff at the hotel greeted her as an old friend and could never do enough for her, and she made conquests wherever she went. Having had a lesson in pronunciation, in order to sing a song in Dutch, she took delight in making a collection of words that struck her as being particularly funny. One of her comical party pieces was a recitation of a number of

Dutch words which, according to her, had to be pronounced with the mouth pulled down at the corners and exaggerated guttural sounds! 'A gorgeous language', she remarked.

After her first visit to America in 1948 Kathleen had signed a contract for tours there in the following three years. And so on the 18th February 1949 she once more took the boat train for Southampton. Before her was a three-months tour, involving journeys from New York to Minnesota, Canada to Cuba. The previous two months had been strenuous. As well as many Christmas-time performances of the *Messiah,* there had been recitals, recordings and a fortnight's visit to Holland. The Atlantic crossing gave her the opportunity to relax: she enjoyed it to the full and wrote: 'I hope I can justify with my singing this luxurious living.'

The *Queen Mary* arrived thirty-six hours late, so Kathleen went straight from the boat to the rehearsal of a concert version of *Orfeo.* She was to sing it at the Town Hall, New York, with Ann Ayars, her Euridice of the previous Glyndebourne season, and was looking forward very much to meeting her again. The role of *Orfeo* was one of her favourites.

While Kathleen was in New York, she rehearsed with Arpad Sandor, the accompanist who was to go on tour with her. To her great joy she also managed to fit in a lesson with Bruno Walter.

A few days later began a very strenuous tour.

> In the train, just somewhere
> past Toronto.
> 11th March 1949.

Dearest Win'fred,

Well, all goes fairly well here still. This is my fourth consecutive night on a train and I'm on another tonight, and if anybody had warned me, I wouldn't have come but, surprisingly enough, I am as perky as old Nick.

After Granville, Ohio, which I spoke about in my letter to Pop, we had a long journey back to New York, arriving about 4.15 p.m., and then another train to Montreal at 11.15 p.m. We arrived there in a snowstorm and I went straight to bed and slept till 1.10 p.m. Imagine! The concert was at three in the afternoon after four nights in a train!! The hall was packed—it was one of the most important concerts—and from the first they purred—so different from Ohio where half the audience were knitting! It was well worth the long journey, and they have booked me again for next year.

We went out for dinner with the President and it was all really lovely. Now we're somewhere north of Lake Erie on our way to Detroit. There's thick snow everywhere and we've just stopped for a moment at London, Ontario!

After a concert in Indianapolis, an awful journey to Pittsburgh, when the engine broke down and the train arrived four hours late, a broadcast and an exciting concert in Pittsburg, she arrived back in New York for a short breathing space.

Dearest Win,

Your airmail written on the 6th March has only just reached me this morning.

I'm so thrilled with your little camera. I had three more films back yesterday and the girl at the shop asked me what camera I was using, she was so impressed! I've even got a squirrel in Central Park.

I'm as fit as a flea—walking a lot when I have an opportunity—drinking *milk* (Gott in Himmel) and I haven't had a cigarette since I left the boat—in fact I'm too good to live (only I hope no one's listening, 'cos I like it just the same!).

A few days later:

I now have six concerts off my chest, and they have all gone very well. Pittsburgh was a huge success, thank goodness!

Bruno Walter is going to play for me in a New York recital next year, as well as Edinburgh and London (Sept. 28th). Isn't that marvellous? He's given me eight new songs to learn, but I do it gladly for him! We've also (Ann and I) been booked for two repeats of *Orfeo* in New York. Klever Us!

The first recital in New York took place on the 28th March in the Town Hall and amongst the audience was a school friend,

Ena Jacobson, who wrote the following article, which was published in the *Northern Daily Telegraph*, Blackburn.[1]

I climbed two flights of stairs to the back of the balcony to stand with others in the Town Hall, New York. I could not get a seat; there was not an empty one in the house. The audience was a show in itself, all types and colours of people, talking many languages——all waiting to hear a Blackburn girl sing to them in one of the most famous concert halls in the world.

Promptly at 8.30 Kathleen Ferrier walked on to the stage followed by her pianist—Arpad Sandor—and a little man ready for his task of turning over the pages.

She looked most regal, in a dress of stiff red satin, trimmed with black, with a beautifully flowing skirt.

First she sang a group of four songs, *Prepare Thyself, Zion* from *Christmas Oratorio*, *Come to me Soothing Sleep*, from *Ottone*, *Have You Seen but a Whyte Lilie Grow* and *Pack Clouds Away*, then six of Schubert's—*Der Musensohn* and *Der Erlkönig* bringing tumultuous applause.

She walked off the stage before the intermission, but the audience would not let her go. The applause was terrific and after reappearing three times, she sang *Who is Sylvia?*

After the interval she first sang *Four Serious Songs* by Brahms, which gave intense satisfaction, but it was her last group of English songs which endeared her to the audience.

When she sang *Love is a Bable* (Parry) there was a ripple of laughter (which Kathleen seemed to enjoy very much) and when she finished with *Oliver Cromwell* there was absolutely deafening applause.

People were standing in their seats and crying 'Bravo' and 'Encore'; she reappeared four times and then to the great satisfaction of the audience sang two Cumberland songs—*A Boating Song* and the *Keel Row*. But this was not enough, and she sang an Irish song. Still the audience was not satisfied, so she sang *My Boy Willie*, which was so popular that she had to sing again—this time another Irish air.

Eventually the only way to persuade the audience to go home, was to put on the house lights and draw the curtain on the stage. All around me I heard people saying, 'Isn't she wonderful? Isn't she goodlooking? I have never heard such singing or seen such poise!'

[1] 6th April 1949. Reproduced by courtesy of the *Northern Daily Telegraph*.

There were young girls and boys—in raptures over the performance and old men and young men, people in evening dress and people in sports clothes, women in the height of fashion and others in shabby clothes—all leaving the concert hall, showing the joy the singing had given to them.

I walked down the staircase which is adorned with the signed photographs of famous musicians from all over the world, who have performed at Town Hall and, hoping to see Kathleen for at least a few minutes, made my way to the stage. There must have been over a hundred people waiting to have at least a glimpse of the singer, to shake her hand, and, if possible, say a few words to her. I watched some flashlight photographs being taken for one of the newspapers—of Kathleen talking to her 'fans'.

There was a long line of people waiting to speak to her—in turn —and eventually I managed to say a few words to her and give congratulations and good wishes from one Blackburnian to another.

She recognised me before I actually spoke and was certainly surprised to find someone from Blackburn in her audience, although one should not be surprised to meet anyone in New York!

How long it took Kathleen to dispose of all her guests I do not know, but she was very hoarse and was presented with a peppermint 'life-saver' by one of her admirers! She said that she was leaving for Ottawa immediately and would give her next recital in New York next year.

Kathleen Ferrier has certainly made a 'hit' here and to do that with a New York audience is something. The people here are very critical, but if they like something, they certainly show it.

It is not often that one sees on a famous concert platform a girl whom one remembers best wearing a gym slip at Blackburn High School!

After the concert Kathleen wrote:

Well, that's over, thank goodness! It was a complete sell-out with about a hundred people sitting on the platform!!

I've never known such applause—I couldn't start for about five minutes! Must have been my red frock! Bruno Walter and Elisabeth Schumann were in the audience, and the clapping almost became a nuisance. I was a bit dry about my throat, but so wet about the torso, I had to keep my frock from sticking to my legs by holding it out in front of me when I walked. People shouted and stamped, but the critics this morning are only lukewarm.

Bruno Walter rang me up—he said the loveliest things and that he was really proud of me. The afternoon papers are better. But I am told these are the most wonderful notices and that I've had the greatest success ever, and, quite honestly, I'm past caring. They were the most lovely audience and they're the ones who've paid for their seats!

Am just dashing to catch a train for Canada and am in the midst of packing. Eee! if mi mother could see me now!!

Well, poppet mine, look after yourself. Will write again soon. Loads of love.

Klever Question Mark Kaff.

and the next day:

Chateau Laurier
Ottawa, Ontario.
30th March 1949.

Off on travels again and have just come overnight from New York via Montreal. Was grey with tiredness after recital, but have been to bed this afternoon and hope I can murmur something tonight! I *do* wonder why I do it sometimes, but wouldn't miss it. I was furious today because when we arrived at noon, they said there wouldn't be a room ready until late afternoon and I enjoyed myself for five minutes telling them what I thought of them, and they had one ready for 1.30!

3rd April.

We're off tomorrow morning at 8 a.m. to La Crosse, Wisconsin. I've had a wonderful day snooping round Chicago with my camera and walking for miles along Lake Michigan. It's been a beautiful day with never a cloud, cold but sunny. I've taken a picture of a Red Indian for our father, but it's only a statue, I'm afraid! Then this afternoon I slept solidly for two hours and tonight I went walking again, and passing a 'flick' I went in and saw Loretta Young in *Mother is a Freshman*. There was a stage show too, and I sat next to the blackest Negro you ever saw, who roared with laughter at everything. I enjoyed him more than the show.

Early in April, Arpad Sandor, her accompanist, became too ill to carry on. From Ottawa on the 11th April she wrote:

On the advice of a woman in Montreal, in whom I have great faith, I have managed to get a man called John Newmark. Aksel Schiøtz and Simon Goldberg have both had him and been thrilled

—the latter is taking him to South Africa—but if he has a sense of humour I can bear almost anything!

I had a wonderful time at Carleton College, Northfield, Minnesota—the head was Professor Gould, who was second-in-command of the Commander Byrd Expedition to the South Pole, and one of the nicest pets you ever did see—both he and his wife incidentally are great friends of Ailie Cullen in Glasgow. The audience were students—mostly voice, and they all clamoured round afterwards, asking me how I did this and that—I felt about ninety—and most of the things I didn't know I'd done! Next morning they took me all round their 'campus'—to the farm, the river and island, and all the different buildings. They are nice, friendly, intelligent creatures these young Americans. At night I went—solo—to dinner with the Goulds and we ate marvellously, and I laughed as I hadn't laughed for ages, and felt a new woman. They saw us on our sleeper and I felt I was leaving my oldest friends!

Kathleen had been very worried by the financial side of this tour. Artists going at that time to the U.S.A. were allowed to take with them only five pounds. When on arrival in New York she found that she was beginning her tour owing a considerable amount of money for advertising, she was appalled. For the first time in her life she was in debt and the thought that if she were ill she would be unable to repay the money made her very miserable. By the time she reached Chicago she had decided that, as she had put it once before at school, 'This is more than flesh and blood can stand!'

15th April 1949.

Dearest Win'fred,

I've just had the time of my life—I've been telling the Chicago manager what I think of him and the whole managerial set-up here—and what's more, I didn't cry!

Mind, it won't make any difference, but at least I've got it off my chest!! I've really been miserable until now with my money disappearing down a drain of advertising and manager's pockets!

I said I wanted to know where, if the concerts were non-profit-making, the money went. I have an average of 3,000 in the audience —which means at least 3,000 dollars and they pay me 800, out of which I pay an accompanist 105—20 per cent. manager's fees—rail travel for two (which is a colossal amount here) hotel, taxis, porters and tips—and income tax! I told him I was the highest paid artist (singer) in England, and was wanted in every country on the Continent—that I hated the halls here—they were too big for recitals, and if I was going to suffer and not enjoy my work, I wanted well paying for it—not go home penniless. Otherwise I would cut down my visits here to the minimum and sing in England where they'd been waiting to get me for three years! I also said I came to this country as an established artist and didn't want to be treated like a beginner, and I told how one of the girls at the office in New York had told me what nail varnish to wear —what hair style—how much eye shadow—the colour of lipstick, and I said I didn't want to outshine Hollywood and remove all signs of character.

I said a lot more for a whole hour-and-a-half—and I feel wonderful. I did say that if American artists came to England we didn't tell them how to dress—nor did we send them to little Muddlecombe to sing for two hours and then be out of pocket. I'm learning to talk straight here—but am becoming hard-boiled on the process. We're firm friends now! But isn't it hard work!

About the same time she received a letter, complaining that she had not been often enough to Holland. In connection with this she wrote:

In 1946 I wasn't suitable for recitals—I knew three songs in German and that was all—my fourth, Erlkönig, I learnt coming to America last year, and the rest I have learnt since. I'm booked up until April 1950. I don't want to miss the *St. Matthew Passion* again. I've sung more in Holland than anywhere—every song I know—and I've only about six weeks in England this year. If I just had to sing, and no visas, taxes and dates to think about, I shouldn't know what to do with myself—but I'd probably sing better!

From Wisconsin she wrote:

Well, your little camera's taking beautiful pictures and its been my main source of enjoyment.

Listen buddy—how do I lose weight. I'm 12 stone 1 lb.!! I got the shock of my life. That's been creeping on for twelve months, so I must do something about it!

I've made some wonderful friends here—I've had women

following me from one concert to the next, two hundred miles apart—and they are the nicest pets and the most generous I could ever wish to meet—so with proper fees it can be wonderful.

When John Newmark arrived they had a rehearsal immediately. From then on her life became easier. Not only had she complete confidence in his playing, but he also took responsibility for travelling and concert arrangements and generally smoothed her path in every possible way. Their first concert was in Battle Creek, Michigan. There was a party afterwards and when it was over Kathleen went wearily to bed—but not to sleep. In the hotel was a grocers' convention, and according to Kathleen's diary there were cans of grape-fruit rolling down the stairs all night. 'Didn't sleep a wink', she wrote.

Each time they arrived at a fresh place, John Newmark made it his business to find out what was to be seen in the neighbourhood. Then he would take Kathleen to the most interesting places, and so she was enabled to see as much as possible with the minimum waste of time and energy. This she appreciated very much. It was also a comfort to have someone look after her, and she had the greatest admiration for his command of languages, his musical culture and his enthusiasm for music.

Writing from Chicago on the 20th April, she said:

John Newmark continues splendidly and we've even had three hours extra good work at my Edinburgh programme on the new German songs—he's German and an excellent coach so is invaluable. It's such a relief—I've learnt six Brahms songs in the last month and I feel so righteous, I'm unbearable.

Some kind people have lent me their apartment complete with cook and maid, on the Lake Shore Drive (frightfully grand) and I've had a splendid three days—that's why I've been able to practice. She also left me four pairs of nylons for my birthday!! The people really are amazingly generous and energetic! We are off tonight to Cape Girardeau in Missouri.

After a concert at Cape Girardeau, and a difficult journey with many changes of train, no porters, and a taxi ride of four miles, they arrived at Danville, Kentucky. Kathleen wrote, 'Funny peculiar hotel with drug store restaurant. Concert in cinema—no dressing room—noisy audience but calmed down.

Man who turned music pages over cried all night! Rush for train—just time for sandwich in milk bar'.

Next day she continued: 'Arrived Columbia 4.45 p.m. Another train for Sumter, arrived 7 p.m. Had to change again. No "redcaps"—in desperation had expensive taxi, forty miles. Had Southern Fried Chicken—very delicious.'

From Florence, S. Carolina, she wrote:

'Looked round shops—bed in afternoon—concert in nicest hall yet acoustically.' It was here that one of the members of the local committee said that 'The President thought they might need some refreshment, and that they had therefore gone to the extra expense of inviting them to a roadhouse dinner.' Kathleen was not only amused by the way this invitation was worded, but fascinated by the Southern accent of the speaker. When she returned home she declared that in the 'deep south' people took a breath between each word, and she repeated this speech for the benefit of her family and friends.

The concert in Havana was memorable. 'Very happy here,' she wrote. In the garden of the British Ambassador's house in Cuba were huge orchids growing on the trunks of the trees. One tree had leaves the size of an umbrella, and Kathleen and John each took one as a souvenir. The leaves were so big that they only just succeeded in packing them into the lids of their suitcases. They did not realise that it is strictly forbidden to take plants into the U.S.A., and when their baggage was examined at the customs, the leaves had to be thrown away.

For a whole afternoon they went sight-seeing in old Havana and while visiting Baccardi's had an opportunity of sampling their famous drink, Daiquiri, a fine rum, which, with a little lemon juice and crushed ice added, is mixed into a delicious foamy drink.

From Cuba Kathleen flew to Miami for a short holiday.

Miami Beach   Monday, 10th May 1949
Dearest Win'fred!

Here I am at last, safely, after flying from Cuba yesterday—I'm almost beginning to enjoy it—and yesterday was quite rough and we had to fasten our belts.

John Newmark has gone to Montreal for ten days, and I'm on

my own. He does play beautifully—does all the dirty work like enquiring for trains and planes, and seeing the piano and stage are all right, etc., bosses me completely, which is quite a new feeling for me! has terrific concentration and absorbs everything he sees and hears and never forgets it again—how I envy him his memory!

I've been in the water this afternoon and it was like a warm bath—it was gorgeous! I'm pink in some amazing places, but feel self-conscious with my lilywhite legs here—with everybody else *dark* mahogany!

Havana was incredible and really tropical and oh, so luxurious! but we had a grand time and the concert went well. The British Ambassador was there, and last Sunday we dined at his house—a palace!

They paid me in cash in Cuba, so I've been having fun—bought two sun-dresses, two pure silks, and a bathing costume—none of the frocks more than £4 10s. each! I leave here on the 17th very early and fly to New York.

                                                    New York
                                                18th May 1949

Dearest Win'fred,

Back home again and they were all thrilled to see me at the Weylin Hotel. Also, all my letters were here from the 28th March!!! 56 of them! I played hell in the office this morning! I'm just beginning to enjoy playing hell! I pointed out that they hadn't put my fee up for next year—got it put up on the instant! My, but isn't it hard work! Only fifty dollars a concert, but better than 'nowt'. Actually, I wouldn't have missed this tour for anything, especially Miami and Cuba, but I don't like being *put on*!

To give me courage I bought a new hat, bag, shoes, stockings and summer nylons and could have coped with a whole board of directors. I have only sagged a little now, having discovered that the tab of my dress had been sticking out at the back of my neck all the time. I *thought* people were looking at me, but I thought it was admiration!! That'll larn me! I bought a navy blue and white spotted pure silk dress for four pounds in Miami, so I bought a little white hat, blue and white shoes, white bag and gloves, and felt real dandy. The white hat has a navy blue veil—very pretty. I gave my black one to a Negro porter in a rushed moment when I hadn't a hand free!

Ooooh! I'd love a black paint box for mi birfday—yes please! Will get on with the other fifty five letters now!

A few days later she wrote:

Dearest Paddy and Pop,

Thank you for all your letters. I can't tell you what a joy it has been to receive them and to know how well you are doing.

I was telling Win in her letter—my earnings were 17,500 dollars (£4,375) and when I've paid my fare (1,000 dollars) and left something here for advertising (1,500 dollars) I shall have just about 1,500 dollars out of 17,500 (£375!)!! Better than a kick in mi nylon pants, but still!! I haven't 'arf worked hard! Have told them to stop advertising, so the 1,500 dollars should be here to come back to, which will be better than starting in debt.

Well, I never expected to reach Louisville. We started off from New York in a downpour of rain—splashed thro' a lake of water on the aerodrome to get to our places and came through a tornado in West Virginia. It rained, it lightened, it leapt up and down, it nearly turned ruddy somersaults, and we were three hours late, and t'was a good job we'd had no lunch or I should have lost it! There were 37 people killed in the tornado and much damage, but the old airplane came down eventually, safely if lopsidedly in the wind! Talk about being glad to be on terra cotta!!

This morning I couldn't raise my head!—it was draughty in the plane and getting wet was very uncomfortable. I've a concert tonight and tomorrow and I've been to an osteopath, but I still can't do my hair or scratch my back!!

But otherwise I'm fine—I've paid my Income Tax (3,500 dollars). I've got my extension as an alien. I've got my sticky labels marked 'Cunard White Star to Europe' and in four days I'll be sticking 'em on and look out, Hampstead, here comes Kaff!

CHAPTER THIRTEEN

Europe

A LARGE black japanned box—the promised birthday present —arrived at Frognal. Kathleen wanted to try her new oil-paints at once. Although a taxi was due to pick her up in about an hour, she squeezed out some colours on to the palette, propped up a canvas board on her dressing table and painted the first object her eyes lighted on—a beige suitcase with a black hat box on top and with an old red plush Teddy bear leaning at the side. Working quickly and with much enjoyment, she finished the picture in about an hour, labelled it 'Ready for off' and called it 'Op. One'.

From the Maitlands' house in Edinburgh she wrote later: 'Could hardly finish breakfast without showing each other's pictures and had session immediately after. Alec has pinched my Op. 1, and hopes our father doesn't mind too much, but he is going to start a picture gallery of Opuses Oneses.'

After her first attempt at painting there were so many engagements that she had to wait until her holiday before she could try again.

On 10th June, 1949 Kathleen flew to Holland. Under the conductorship of Pierre Monteux, she was to take part in a production of *Orfeo* at the Holland Festival. There was to be a fortnight of rehearsals before the first night on 24th June, and she was very anxious for her sister to come to Holland for the occasion. When Win wrote that she was doubtful of being able to get leave from school, the following reply came:

Now look 'ere, our Winnie! Peter Diamand's going to be disappointed, cross and put out if you don't come to Amsterdam for

Orfeo, specially as he is arranging a Saturday and Sunday performance for your benefit.

Now here's an idea! and be honest and tell me if you don't
like it—catch morning plane Friday, lunch in Amsterdam—stay
three nights—fly back Monday morning. You could be in school
by 2 p.m. The journey and hotel expenses would be my birthday
present to you with my love. Howzat? Go on, be a devil!

It's just grand here—I'm full of steaks, eggs, sole fried in butter,
salads, Bols and Chianti and surrounded with flowers. I've had a
running cold, but it's only improved my resonators!

Look after yourself—loads of love. Kaff.

This of course, was more than Win could resist. Mr. and Mrs.
Maitland also decided to join them and, in order to be in time
for the first night, undertook *their* first journey by air.

A few days before Win was due to leave for Holland,
Kathleen wrote:

All goes well here—haven't rehearsed with Monteux yet, but
he should be lovely to work with. Had my first night out last
night and went to *Manon*—it was excellent.

If you could get any cigs. would you bring some, love? The
manager is pining for some English ones.

I may not be able to meet you because of rehearsals, but the bus
will bring you from the airport, almost next door to the hotel—
I'm yearning to take you to a Dutch meal! Don't forget your
camera and there are some films in my wardrobe.

There followed a memorable week-end for Win: her first
journey abroad since the war, her first experience of flying, and
the airport bus being met in Amsterdam by a beaming Kathleen.
They went at once, to 'the little restaurant round the corner',
where she was now almost one of the family, and after a sump-
tuous lunch Kathleen rested, while Win met the Maitlands who
arrived in the afternoon.

That evening, there was the thrilling atmosphere of a great
occasion in the Opera House. As Queen Juliana came in,
accompanied by Prince Bernhard, the audience rose and sang
the Dutch National Anthem. Then Gluck's wonderful music
began. As Sir Steuart Wilson had said—the ideal performance of

this beautiful opera can only be experienced in dreams—but there were many moments of beauty in this performance, and at the end there were scenes of great enthusiasm from the audience.

Afterwards, there was a banquet at which all those connected with the opera were present. It went on for hours, with delicious food appearing on the plates every time one looked away, and many speeches, all in English, from the members of the committee. 'Makes you ashamed of being such a lazy linguist,' said Kathleen.

The following day, she went with the Maitlands and Win to see the Stedelijk Museum. Mr. and Mrs. Maitland knew many of the pictures well, and now that they had all begun to try to paint, they appreciated even more the achievements of the great artists whose work hung there.

The performances continued to go well. Kathleen wrote:

Last *Orfeo* tonight. I think I am very good now in it!

A few days later:

WELL! Life gets *more* hectic here, but I couldn't miss the opportunity of hearing the Vienna Opera each night! *Il Seraglio* was wonderful (Krips conducting) but *Rosenkavalier* last night— Phew!—it goes on for hours and though the production was wonderful, I'm completely unimpressed, unmoved and rather bored.

The Monteuxs went yesterday—he weeping I'm told—because the orchestra and chorus came to the hotel and played *Carmen*, *For he's a jolly good fellow* and many more things. It was like a scene in a film, with crowds standing all round and police guarding them! Dear, sweet Holland! Have to rehearse *Orfeo*, still learn mi Bach— not to mention B.B., which I still haven't started on! The Maitlands go tomorrow—the Christies arrived yesterday—it's all much too social to work, but awful nice.

'Mi Bach' that she still had to learn, was the *Solo Cantata No. 169*, which she was to sing as well as Purcell's *Te Deum* and Bach's *Magnificat* in the Concertgebouw, with the Netherlands Bach Society, conducted by Dr. van der Horst. The 'B.B., which I still haven't started on' was Benjamin Britten's *Spring Symphony*—the first performance of which was due to take place later. Two days before the première she wrote:

Working like a nigger at the Britten—I can get my 'oo' but I'm bothered if I can get mi 'cuck'. Poor Kaff! I'm a shadow!

The world première of the *Spring Symphony* took place on 14th July 1949. Benjamin Britten wrote:[1] 'I had Kathleen very much in mind when I wrote the long serious setting of a poem by W. H. Auden, which is the central piece of the work. Her beautiful dark voice and serious mien, together with her impeccable intonation, made a great impression in this sombre movement. Also memorable in this most wonderful of first performances (played superbly by the Concertgebouw Orchestra under der van Beinum) was her gaiety in the trio of birds in *Spring, the Sweet Spring,* along with Jo Vincent and Peter Pears.'

Kathleen enjoyed this performance and was particularly intrigued by the use made of the boys' voices and the spirited way in which the choir of schoolboys whistled and sang.

There was less than a fortnight at home, during which time she gave a broadcast recital and sang the Brahms's *Four Serious Songs* at a Promenade Concert, before she was packing to go to Switzerland. After all her hard work, Kathleen had originally planned to have the whole of August free. Then she had heard from Bruno Walter. He was returning after an absence of twelve years to the Salzburg Festival and was conducting *Das Lied von der Erde*. He had asked her to take part in it, and there had been no question of a refusal. She loved working with him and was honoured by his confidence in her. And so it was arranged that she and Win should have a ten-day holiday in Switzerland before going to Salzburg. Kathleen, who was desperately tired, was unusually quiet on the journey, but as the funicular lifted them to the airy heights of Wengen, her spirits rose. From the balconies of their rooms were wonderful views of the valley and snow-capped mountains, including the Jungfrau. Much time was spent on the balcony, lying in the sun and painting. Kathleen, generally so sociable, did not want to make friends with the people in the hotel. She needed rest, peace and an opportunity to restore her forces.

Mornings were spent in painting, and as it seemed a pity to

[1] *Kathleen Ferrier: A Memoir.* Hamish Hamilton.

miss an opportunity for sunbathing at the same time, the choice of subject was influenced to some extent by the position of the sun and the part of the anatomy most in need of toasting. 'I've got burnt everywhere except my back legs,' said Kathleen, 'and they are still lily-white—I feel ashamed of them.' In the afternoon she rested and then after an early cup of tea, she and Win set out for a long walk. Through the pine-woods out on to little green hills and under the shadows of the great mountains. Sometimes they walked for miles in companionable silence, sometimes Kathleen sang softly:

> Die Sonne scheidet hinter dem Gebirge
> In alle Täler steigt der Abend nieder
> Mit seinen Schatten, die voll Kühlung sind.[1]

Although by the end of the holiday Kathleen was looking and feeling much better, she really needed a longer time to rest. As the train made its way into Austria, she became more and more depressed. Knowing that she was the first English singer to be invited to the Salzburg Festival, she felt her responsibility keenly. She would be singing in German to German-speaking audiences, audiences moreover steeped in the tradition of previous performances of Mahler's work. She was anxious to justify Bruno Walter's faith in her.

When at last the train stopped at Salzburg it was raining heavily. Kathleen and Win were met by one of the festival officials and taken to their hotel. They were surprised to find that it had no lounge and very little comfort, not realising until later that Salzburg, being part of the American zone, was occupied by the military, who had taken over most of the big hotels. This one was famous as an eating house, but the smell of frying onions permeated it, striking an almost physical blow when the bedroom door opened in the morning.

Kathleen was delighted next day to find that Victor Olof, the musical director of Decca, was staying in the same hotel. Knowing Salzburg well, he was able to show many interesting places which otherwise they would have missed.

[1] The sun is setting behind the mountains,
Evening with its deep cool shadows
Descends in every valley.

At first, however, she was concentrating all attention on the forthcoming performance of *Das Lied von der Erde*. After the first rehearsal she felt much better: to be working again with Bruno Walter filled her with joy. The playing of the Vienna Philharmonic Orchestra she thought was superb, and the fact that the members applauded her when she finished singing cheered her heart. 'If the *orchestra* thinks you are good, then you really *are* good.'

The first performance at 11 o'clock in the morning of 21st August was exciting, but the second one, the following evening, touched rare heights of musical feeling and interpretation. Kathleen knew that she had sung well; and the press reports reassured her.

'The young Kathleen Ferrier justifies Professor Walter's gift for discovering singers', said the *Wiener Tageblatt* of 23rd August 1949, and in the *Presse*: 'Her voice, which I should like to compare with organ tones, is a very satisfying sound. Apart from this, she gave in her interpretation the ecstatic expression which is the important element in Mahler—her achievement can be put side by side with the best representatives of this part.'

After this, Kathleen was all gaiety and out for enjoyment. She and Win heard performances of *Orfeo* and *Der Rosenkavalier*, they went sight-seeing with Bruno Walter's daughter and they took a car with Victor Olof and made a tour of the lovely Salz-kammergut.

On 5th October 1949, Kathleen, with Phyllis Spurr, set off for a second visit to Scandinavia. The first engagement was for a broadcast of *Che Faro* and Brahms's *Alto Rhapsody* from Copenhagen. The plane was late in arriving. A choir and orchestra were waiting to rehearse. Officials came forward carrying bouquets of flowers and then, while the other passengers were held back, Kathleen and Phyllis were whisked off through the customs and driven at top speed to the concert hall. This delighted Kathleen, who never became blasé about such incidents.

Her broadcasts in Scandinavia were treated as great occasions : the officials of the radio stations looked after her with the greatest attention and entertained her royally afterwards.

For her first concert in Copenhagen, a hall holding about 500 people was chosen: all seats were sold. When she returned to give a second concert, a larger hall holding 1900 was filled, people sitting in the gangways and on the platform. A third concert was held to accommodate those who had failed to get seats, and this too was sold out. The organisers wanted to arrange a fourth one, but other engagements made it impossible.

In Denmark Kathleen, coached phonetically by the daughter of the house where she was staying, learnt a Danish song in a day and sang it from memory. In Oslo too, she learnt one written by Jensen and sang it in Norwegian after studying it for a few hours. On this occasion there was no hall for a concert, so the Broadcasting Association lent one for a recital before an invited audience. Immediately afterwards she and Phyllis heard the recording, and Kathleen was filled with horror and wanted to do it again. She felt sure that she could sing it much better the second time.

Once when they took a taxi in Stockholm and asked for the stage door of the Concert Hall, the driver said: 'Ah, you must be Miss Ferrier. What are you singing tonight?' When she told him the names of the Lieder, he quoted some of the words.

The audiences in Scandinavia were a great joy. They knew and understood what she was singing. When at the end of a concert she had sung five or six encores, the piano had to be shut and the lights lowered before they would go home.

There were two separate recital programmes for this tour.

One was:

Schubert.	*Die Junge Nonne*
	Du bist die Ruh
	Du liebst mich nicht
	Der Tod und das Mädchen
	Suleika 1.
	Romance from 'Rosamunde'
Schumann.	*Frauenliebe und Leben*

Brahms:	*Immer leiser wird mein Schlummer*
	Am Sonntag Morgen
	Wir wandelten
	Botschaft
	Von ewiger Liebe

The other:

Handel:	*How changed the vision*
	Like as the love-lorn turtle
Purcell:	*Hark the ech'ing air*
	Mad Bess
Antonio Lotti:	*Pur dicesti, O bocca bella*
Monteverdi:	*Lasciatemi morire*
Gluck:	*Che farö senza Euridice* (Orpheus)
Hugo Wolf:	*Verborgenheit*
	Der Gärtner
	Auf ein altes Bild
	Auf einer Wanderung
Parry:	*Love is a bable*
Stanford:	*A soft day*
Britten:	*Flower Song* (Rape of Lucretia)
	The Ash Grove
	Oliver Cromwell

Towards the end of the tour she wrote from Aarhus:

We've just rolled off the boat from Copenhagen and are about to go to bed for the day! It's raining hard and rather miserable, so a book and bed seem the answer. No concert until tomorrow night!

This seems to have been our first pause in the rush, but it's been wonderful everywhere with sold-out halls and superlative criticisms. K.K.! There were no fur coats in Oslo, but I've got two lovely blue foxes for—well, I'll let you guess when you've seen them. Phyllis had hers made into a cape and it's lovely, and I've got two tiny minks for decoration on a coat—lovely dark brown.

We flew back from Stockholm to Copenhagen in the oldest Czecho-Slovak 'plane you ever saw—but we made it—but the next morning I woke up and couldn't lift my head again—there'd been a hellofadraft—so I've been having beautiful massage—they come to the house (I was staying with the manager in Copenhagen) and pommel one for an hour for seven shillings!! The reason for my fat right arm is rheumatic, the man says, and he says I ought to have massage weekly. So I'm going to try to find someone to come to the flat now and again—it's a wonderful excuse to have massage. At the concert in Copenhagen the other night I could bend down but could hardly get back, so they had to be content with superior nods of the cranium! They went mad, and I couldn't go on till we repeated *Botschaft*. I've never had that happen before. Phyllis has been fine—she's spoiled me and looked after me and she's played well. She's thrilled with her cape.

The British Ambassador gave a reception for me yesterday in his gorgeous home and I went dolled up in my grey frock and furs and felt wonderful.

My last concert's Friday in Copenhagen and we'll be home Saturday—4.30–5 p.m. *D.V.*

A week later, Sunday evening 6th November, Kathleen boarded the train ferry—bound, for the first time, for Paris. Under the auspices of L'Association Française d'Action Artistique a recital had been arranged to take place in the Salle Gaveau. Her diary read: 'Arrived Paris 9.30. Rehearsed 11. Lunch, sleep, interview. Cocktail party. Rehearsal after. Good dinner.' The following day: 'Rained hard but gazed at wondrous shops—rehearsed, lunched and slept.'

Her programme consisted of German Lieder—six by Schubert, the *Frauenliebe und Leben* of Schumann and six by Brahms. She was accompanied by André Collard. The report in *Paroles Françaises* for 11th November 1949 said 'This English singer conquered Paris with the opening bars of her Schubert Lieder.'

SALZBURG, 1947
On the steps of the Mozarteum with Victor Olof

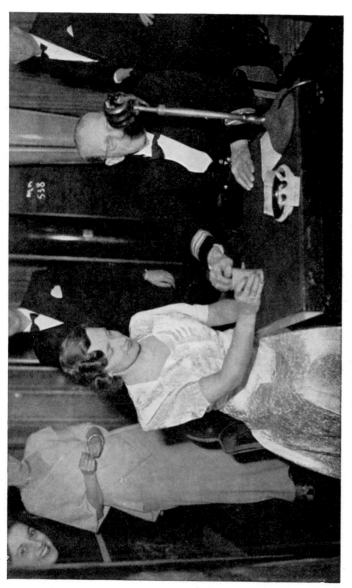

ON BOARD THE *QUEEN MARY*, 1948

TOURING IN AMERICA
With Arpad Sandor

AT FROGNAL, 1948

IN MONTREAL
With John Newmark's cat

WITH (RIGHT TO LEFT)
ANNE AYARS, MRS.
SCHNEIDER AND HANS
SCHNEIDER

Taken by Kathleen with
a self-timer

PORTRAIT BY CECIL BEATON, 1951

CHAPTER FOURTEEN

Ladies and Gentlemen

CHRISTMAS 1949 saw Kathleen on board the *Queen Elizabeth* bound for America. She was looking forward with pleasure to this tour; there would be happy reunions with many good friends; she would be working once more with Bruno Walter; John Newmark would be playing for her.

From New York, 27th December 1949:

> Arrived to find a note from Columbia to say John Newmark, being a Canadian, had been refused permission to work in the U.S.A.!!! So got to work—contacted lawyers, British Embassy and Canadian Embassy, and this morning I've had news that the original decision may be cancelled and that—fingers crossed—he may be allowed to play for me. I shall know definitely tonight or tomorrow! Hardly dare breathe.

A few days later:

> John Newmark got here finally—it's cost me £11 in telephone calls, and him 500 dollars for lawyers—but he's playing *quite* beautifully and I wish you could hear him.
>
> Our first concert went well and the second miserably—just the difference in small things of hall, organisers and thoughtfulness—so perhaps if it goes alternately, tomorrow won't be so bad after all!
>
> Ruth Draper has been a peach—and had a lovely party for me on New Year's Day, when I sang and Johnny played—we tried most of our programmes out on the few guests there—so haven't much to rehearse now. She's a charmer and we're just buddies!

The party on New Year's Day was followed by a letter from Ruth Draper:

My dearest Kathleen,

You can't think of the pleasure you gave me and the others last night—far more than pleasure—a deep and lovely impression of true beauty and lasting haunting memory. My room has been consecrated by many lovely hours of music, by the gathering of fine spirits and friends that I cherish—you added so much to what means more than anything in life—the beauty of the human spirit conveyed through art, to remind us always of the heights to which we can soar—and of the best in us. Bless you for your simple and humble generous giving of your gift—it was a perfect beginning to the New Year, and I hope your happiness in your work and the joy it gives us all will continue to flower and grow.

My warm greetings and thanks to Mr. Newmark for his wonderful playing of those great songs. God speed you dear—and think of me as your devoted friend,

Ruth.

While she was in New York Kathleen had some singing lessons. There were three notes in her voice, middle E, F, G, about which she felt dissatisfied, and on her previous visit Madame Clytie Mundy had helped her. She had another lesson and found it 'a wonderful help', and when she returned to New York later had several more.

The tour that followed was particularly successful—the travelling was not unduly difficult, the concerts went well, and there was some time to go sight-seeing occasionally or to a film. One evening Johnny took her to one which he had heard was good. It was called *Since You Went Away*. After a while he began to wonder whether Kathleen had got a cold, but he soon realised that she was weeping, and when they came out she said, 'Never do that to me again. I just can't stand a sad film.'

In the train on the way from Chicago to Santa Fé:

Last week we were in Nebraska when it was I don't know how many below zero, and now we're just steaming through New Mexico, where the sun is so hot that I've to keep the blind down in my roomette! We've been going for hours through desert, with just occasionally a horse or a few cows and an awful lot of dust. Johnny and I have just had breakfast on the train and, after a jolly good sleep last night—ten hours—I am feeling very well, thank you! Hope you both are too.

At La Crosse I did the Brahms's *Alto Rhapsody* and Pergolesi's *Stabat Mater* with their choir and offered to do another group, as they were paying me a lot and brought Johnny from Chicago, so they were all thrilled and pleased with me and pleased with themselves for tackling such nice works, so all was very well, I had a bouquet of red and yellow roses from a millionaire admirer, and one of lovely pink ones from the choir, so I was a real prima donna. I stayed with Mrs. Cress and her eyes just popped all week-end with excitement.

We have been on this train since 1 p.m. yesterday and it's nearly noon today, but it's so comfortable and the food is so good that I'm loath to get out, and that's a change!

Our concerts are going beautifully—and the reviews we've seen so far have been fine, so all's well and we're as happy as larks. Johnny's playing gets better, which I didn't think was possible, and we get on very well.

I have an extra broadcast in San Francisco on 5th February but shall probably be coming back to Los Angeles, so my letter addresses will stand.

A postcard from Santa Fé:

26th January, 1950.

Isn't this a lovely place to be staying? We're 7,000 feet high and my breath's coming in short pants, but it's lovely. Hot sun, blue sky and today, snow. Everything Mexican and Indian and very interesting. Go tomorrow to Arizona and stay in a ranch house!! Then on to California to stay with Ann's and Dottie's parents and then at Bruno Walter's. Lucky, ain't I?

On arrival, she found awaiting her the letter from Bruno Walter which is reproduced on the next page:

Beverly Hills, January 26th 1950

Dear Kathleen!

Welcome in my house! Please feel entirely at home in it – everything is at your disposal: the house, the piano, the music, the books and of course also the cars, wherever you want to go. Adolf and Fanny will do their best, to make your stay pleasant and comfortable and Fanny in particular will provide for pleasures of your palate. By the way: Adolf is really an excellent chauffeur and you may feel safe when he is at the wheel. – I presume you will spend as restful a time as possible in my house and fully understand if you do not want to talk or make acquaintances.

With affectionate greetings and "auf Wiedersehen")

yours sincerely

Bruno Walter

From Bruno Walter's house she wrote on 3rd February:

All is simply perfect here. I have started my ten days off now and shall be here until the 13th at Bruno Walter's.

He has a lovely house with swimming pool and man and wife to look after me. All the Walters are in New York—but Lotte rang me this morning to see if I was all right—three thousand miles! Each room has its own bathroom with the most wonderful plumbing. This afternoon Johnny and I have been all round Bel Air to the top of the mountain in the open car to see the wonderful homes and views—also to the Hollywood Bowl that holds 20,000 people. The sun is glorious and the oranges are on the trees and it all just makes your mouth water.

Last night we performed in a lovely hall of a university. They (the audience) stood and shouted at the end and it really did go well. Unfortunately, Rodzinski was conducting at the same time, so there isn't a single criticism.

The people are so kind, it's almost overwhelming. Fanny, the wife here, has just brought me Bruno's typewriter to use—so I should get on better now. I have a stack of letters waiting to be answered—so this should help. There is no exclamation mark though, and I am lost without one for all my adventures.

I gave John and Leon the new *Kindertotenlieder* records for their Christmas present, as I had promised them—and he said he would ask zou to hear them—but with going into hospital he couldn't make it, so if zou have a minute to go and see him, he'd be verz thrilled, and zou could hear them. Thez only came the day before I left—I hope zou liked them, tho' the first record is not the one to be published as I run out of breath in one phrase. (Gee—I'm getting mi ZZZZs mixed up, ain't I?) I do hope you like the records —I was rather pleased with them myself, for once, but will probably change my mind when I hear them again.

Johnny is fine—his playing gets better and better—I think he must be one of the finest in the world, and he enjoys it so.

Well, love—this is all for now—look after yourself and I do hope the weather cheers up—I wish you could share some of this sun— p'raps one of these days—who knows?? Much love to you—God bless.

Kaff.

During her stay in Beverly Hills, Kathleen made the most of opportunities for sight-seeing. She was fascinated by the

Turnabout Theatre where there are two platforms and the seat can be turned to face either way. There were puppets at one end and a variety show, featuring Elsa Lanchester, at the other.

A week was spent with Ann Ayars' parents. Of this Ann wrote: 'What impressed mother most about Kath was her almost childlike capacity for enjoying such simple things—like wading in the Pacific. My parents took her and Johnny down to Laguna Beach and almost before they could stop, Kath was out of the car and had run way ahead of them down to the shore, had thrown her shoes and stockings to the breeze and was in the water, splashing and laughing like a child. Daddy had to run to collect her things, or the wind would have blown her stockings away, but Kath didn't even notice, she was having such a wonderful time in the water all by herself. They were so tickled with her.'

After this delightful holiday, Kathleen felt in very good form for three concert performances of *Orfeo* in San Francisco. When John Newmark went to hear the rehearsal, there were only two other people in the auditorium—a man and a woman. When Kathleen had sung her first few bars, the woman threw back her head and said, 'My God, what a voice! and what a face!' It was the great coloured singer, Marian Anderson, who had stayed on an extra day to hear the rehearsal. Afterwards she and Kathleen were introduced and Kathleen was thrilled to meet one whose records she admired so much.

All the notices were enthusiastic on this occasion with head-lines such as 'Standing Ovation accorded Ferrier's San Francisco Debut'.

Her diary reads:

February 15th. *Orfeo* went beautifully—Mrs. Monteux gave me a lovely pearl ring. Lucky Kaff! Flowers and flowers—real prima donna!

February 17th. Went well again. Reception at Yacht Club and lovely Chinese dinner over the longest bridge in the world.

February 18th. Concert went even better! So happy. Spoiled to death!

Sir John Barbirolli had asked Kathleen to learn Chausson's *Poème d'Amour et de la Mer* in French, so that she could sing it with him the following year. About this time came a letter from Mrs. Tillett asking her whether or not she would accept this engagement. Feeling that she ought to have time to study in France before undertaking such a work, Kathleen was inclined to refuse, even though she was most anxious to do as Sir John wished. When she talked it over with John Newmark, however, he urged her to accept, offering to coach her in the French text while on their tour. After some hesitation, she sent the following cable:

Accept Chausson. Tell Sir John to play loudly to cover my Lancashire accent.

Kathleen and John Newmark were able to work a good deal as they travelled about, and on the 23rd February she wrote in her diary: 'On train all day—lovely. Did a lot of work on Chausson.'

John Newmark also wrote to a French friend, Paul Roussel in Montreal, asking him to make a record of the poems, reading them slowly so that every syllable could be heard. When they reached Montreal, Kathleen was delighted to find this record waiting for her. She took it home and practised a good deal with it.

In Weaton, Illinois, she was able to attend a concert conducted by Bruno Walter and, after giving two more recitals herself, she and Johnny went to see Niagara Falls. 'Very fine,' she wrote, 'and nice luncheon overlooking them. Icy cold weather.' They returned to Montreal for a recital. Afterwards, she said to Johnny, 'Was it all right?', and when he replied that it certainly was, she said, 'I'm so glad. I didn't want to let you down in your home town!'

At the beginning of March 1950 Kathleen had a letter from Mrs. Tillett asking whether she would consider taking the part of Nicklaus in the film *Tales of Hoffman*. She replied:

My dear Emmie,

I am a diva of the deepest and dirtiest dye for not having written e'er this. My only excuse is that I have been a dam' industrious diva for the last two weeks, and I hope you'll forgive me. I will take your questions in turn and see what happens!

Me in a film? 'Pon mi soul! I don't know the part or if it

is suitable—and could the cameraman remove my curves?—but I couldn't give a definite answer just now until I know more about it. It would be interesting if it were rewarding—musically and financially!

After looking at the part and taking into consideration her long list of engagements for the coming twelve months, she decided not to accept this offer.

From St. John, New Brunswick, she wrote to Win:

11th March, 1950.

I'm sorry I haven't written for a while, but have never stopped since San Francisco. Just came here from Montreal and have a concert in four hours time. Came straight to bed for my afternoon siesta off the train, so haven't seen anything! Montreal was wonderful —notices just raving. I'm so pleased as they are all such poppets there. Haven't shopped yet, but going to in New York or Chicago. Is there anything you want especially?

Have you ever had the whiskers in your nose freeze? Well I have—all these last few days in Montreal—it's been 10 degrees below freezing—give me California!

All's wonderfully well—keep fingers crossed for 17th *Orfeo*— 19th recital with Bruno Walter—hope it is with you too. See you soon.

After a concert at St. John, N.B. she went on to Moncton, where there was some difficulty with the plumbing. In her diary was an entry—'Couldn't have a bath—water icy cold!'— then, next day—'Not true! Cold water tap marked Hot and Hot Cold! Didn't discover it for a long time. Ha! Clean again!'

The next day she left for New York and wrote: 'Have developed a tickling throat; hope its only morning dryness from this over heating.' There was no further mention of any throat trouble, and the concert performance of *Orfeo*, conducted by Thomas Scherman, and with Ann Ayars as Euridice, was, according to the critics, a memorable one.

At Hunter College, New York, she gave a recital with Bruno Walter, on March 19, the programme of which was as follows:

I

Die Junge Nonne
Romance, from 'Rosamunde'
Der Musensohn   Schubert
Wanderers Nachtlied
Du liebst mich nicht
Suleika

II

Frauenliebe und Leben   Schumann
  Seit ich ihn gesehen
  Er, der Herrlichste von allen
  Ich kann's nicht fassen
  Du Ring an meinem Finger
  Helft mir, ihr Schwestern
  Süsser Freund, du blickest
  An meinem Herzen
  Nun hast du mir den ersten Schmerz getan

INTERMISSION

III

Immer leiser wird mein Schlummer
Der Tod, das ist die kühle Nacht
Am Sonntag Morgen   Brahms
Wir wandelten
Botschaft
Von ewiger Liebe

Chicago,   24th March, 1950.

Haven't written for an age but have had my busiest time to
date and everything important. All's gone well in spite of draughts
in train and a stiff neck—have just finished my second concert
here and it's been a great success—will enclose a cutting. Off to
Toronto for last concert and then I shall be on the boat on

Wednesday night. It couldn't have been a lovelier tour and I haven't so far (fingers crossed) had a single adverse criticism, but some of the most glowing I've ever had.

Bruno Walter has asked me to do a recital with him in Salzburg the middle of August, if it doesn't clash with Edinburgh—so I should, shouldn't I?

In horrible rush. Hope all's well. (Feeling rather self-satisfied today, but I'll soon lose it!!).

On 4th April she arrived home.

Some time later, she was the guest of honour at a luncheon and wrote afterwards in her diary, 'Made a shocking red-faced speech':

Ladies and Gentlemen,

I should like to say thank you to you all for the great honour you have paid me today.

I must warn you that I am making my debut as an after-luncheon speaker and am more nervous than when I had my first broadcast many years ago in Newcastle, singing *The End of a Perfect Day*. When coming to the end of a perfect luncheon the obvious thing to say would be that I am too full for words, but I do thank my friends here who have proposed my health and said so many complimentary things.

I have been asked if I would say a word or two about my American tour, and to start with I must say the thing that gives me so much pleasure is the voyage, which after a hectically busy time in this country and in Europe is five days of sheer luxury. Five days of no telephones or letters and every excuse for staying in bed, especially if the ship rolls.

My three months this year have taken my pianist and me to many lovely places. New York for three concerts, Pennsylvania, Tennessee, New Mexico, Arizona, Los Angeles, San Francisco, Chicago, Toronto, Montreal and many other smaller places. I can honestly say I haven't a single bad memory. I've caught all the right trains—the halls on the whole were quite good—some of them superb, like the San Francisco Opera House and the Chicago Orchestra Hall—one uncomfortable moment was in Santa Fe, where we were 8,000 feet above sea level and when, for the first half of the programme at any rate, I had the greatest difficulty in breathing because of the rarified atmosphere.

The audiences were most receptive and were delighted if I

explained some of the German songs because of my English-cum-Lancashire accent!

One always hears of Americans coming here and saying, 'Aren't your policemen wonderful'—I feel I should say to them 'Isn't your plumbing wonderful', because wherever I went—in the smallest hotels I always had a room with a bath, and a cupboard or closet long enough to hold my evening dresses. The train travel on main lines is superb with the best meals one could possibly hope for.

This time, too, I had a superb accompanist, who not only played beautifully, but did all the organising of trains, checking and tipping and looking after our numerous bags, so all I had to do was to get to a place and sing as well as I knew how. This organising just made all the difference to my peace of mind and was the main cause of the pleasure of the whole trip.

We did about twenty-three concerts in the three months and made lovely programmes of Bach, Handel, Purcell, Schubert, Schumann, Brahms and Mahler, Elizabethan songs, some contemporary English and folk songs, and I managed to do a little studying as well—usually in the trains.

I had two weeks holiday in Beverly Hills and was a guest in Bruno Walter's house. This was just superb—the sun shone and I was taken round to see the coast and the old missions of California, the orange and lemon groves, and also to Edward G. Robinson's house. He has a most wonderful collection of French paintings.

We came back from California over the Rockies to Chicago and then Canada—now back into winter woollies after sunbathing in January in Arizona and California. We were taken to see the Niagara Falls which is certainly a wonderful sight, but rather spoiled by factories and ugly buildings.

Our last concert was in Toronto, and I had just time to catch a night train—pay a large amount of Income Tax in New York, hastily buy a few nylons and catch the boat back. I even had a cheque in my pocket of dollars for Britain—I don't suppose there will be many left when the tax has been taken off it at this end too, but it made my bank manager smile. He said what a grand job I was doing, bringing dollars into the country, but I think he should have said—what a lucky person you are to be so spoiled, to see so many wonderful places and be *paid* for doing it.

On the *Queen Elizabeth* again—five lovely days—and home to a green England, with the blossom looking more lovely than I've ever seen it and, despite the plumbing, the steaks, the nylons, and the many wonderful friends I left behind, it was good to be home.

CHAPTER FIFTEEN

Conscience Professionelle

O N the 5th June 1950 Kathleen set off for Vienna to take part
in the Bach Festival. She was very much looking forward
to singing in the *St. Matthew Passion,* the *Magnificat* and the
Mass in B Minor.

Everything fine here, Karajan very pleased with me—first
performance tomorrow—*wish* you could hear it. T'will be broadcast
—perhaps you will. Weather simply superb and food superber!
Victor Olof here, being absolute angel. Going to hear Krips
recording tonight—then on to dinner with them both.

A week later:

All's well. Victor Olof and his three engineers have been perfect
pets and we have lunched together each day, and Victor has come
for me after a concert to rescue me from the terrific crowds of
autograph hunters—they're worse than in England. The Krips have
been pets too and we've seen a lot of them.
My last concert is tonight—*B Minor Mass*—the other two safely
and successfully over—and I've been asked back for a recital.
It's been terrifically hot—lovely for lounging but a bit much
in a crowded concert hall. It's rather depressing—there are still
uniforms of four armies about and many beggars and lame, halt
and blind.

Later Kathleen said that this performance of the Bach *Mass in
B Minor* in Vienna was one of the greatest experiences of her life.
The choir and orchestra were superb, she said, they inspired the
soloists.
The following is a translation of a letter she received:

Der Präsident der Gesellschaft der Musikfreunde in Wien.

Wien, den. 16. Juni 1950.

1, Bösendorferkrasse 12.

Dear Miss Ferrier,

The Presidents of the 'Society of Friends of Music' wish to express to you, dear Miss Ferrier, their most heartfelt thanks for your participation in the International Bach Festival of 1950. The wonderful reception which your high artistry obtained from the public was equally felt by the Directors and Presidents of the Society of Friends of Music. We must tell you that not for many years have we been enabled to hear the musical parts interpreted by you in such perfect form. You have, my dear Miss Ferrier, contributed so greatly to the result of our Bach Festival, we wish to add to the thanks already expressed our hopes that you will once again next year be able to give us your collaboration.

In the hopes that we shall soon be enabled to welcome you in Vienna, we remain,

Das Präsidium
der
Gesellschaft der Musikfreunde in Wien.

From Vienna to Zurich, where she wrote:

My concert here is tonight and I shall be relieved when it's over because my bill is terrific—but it's worth it—it's so comfortable. I leave here on Thursday lunchtime for Milan.

Kleiber, whom I was rather dreading, as I had heard he was such a stickler, is a fine conductor and cancelled my final rehearsal this morning as he was so happy! I hope he is as pleased at the concert tonight!

The impresario tells me I'm not allowed to spend so much of my fee, as a part of it *Must* go back to England and I'm only *just* going to have enough to pay my bill and will be counting every franc until I leave. *Honestlee*!

From Zurich Kathleen went on to Milan, where she was met by her friend, Hans Schneider, and by the Vienna manager, armed with a bouquet. There were two free days before the concert so she was able to go sightseeing.

'Had a lovely day with Hans', she wrote. 'Heard the *Missa Solemnis*—Schwarzkopf especially fine.'

The performance of the Bach Mass in La Scala was memorable.

Kathleen was thrilled to be singing there and when, at the end of the *Agnus Dei,* she sat down, some of the audience were in tears.

When she returned home, many business letters awaited her. To one from Mrs. Tillett she replied:

3rd September, 1950.

My dear Emmie,

Here are a few answers to your queries, luv:

Worthing. Brahms Rhapsody in English (Novello)

English Group with Arthur Wayne.

> 'Love is a bable'—Parry
> 'A soft Day'—Stanford
> 'The Fidgety Bairn'—arr. Robertson
> 'Ca' the Yowes'—arr. Jacobson
> 'The Spanish Lady'—arr. Hughes.

I could rehearse Friday and Saturday, 22nd and 23rd. If they want something more solid—e.g. Lieder—will change, but thought this might cheer things up!

May 28th. Elgar—Sea Pictures.

Only sheer love for *you*, Emmie, makes me acquiesce, as the bishop said to the actress!

I'm sorry I can't sing the Verdi Requiem—it breaks mi bloomin' heart, but it's no good—it's too high.

The more I see of opera, the less I want to take part in it—except *Orfeo*—I think I'll have a rest in May.

Would love to take Ernest Lush with me to Scandinavia and agree to his fee—I don't want him to reduce it. Would prefer not to go to Aberdeen May 20th—too big a jump in between Cambridge and Peterborough.

Think that is all for the moment. Much love,

Kathleen.

On 18th September 1950 she gave a broadcast recital of Brahms's *Lieder*, accompanied by Frederick Stone. In reply to a letter from Hans Oppenheim she wrote:

My dear Oppi,

What a lovely letter—I am so glad I didn't let you down completely—that would never do.

Actually, one run through with a pianist is impossible—and all on the day of the broadcast. Usually I manage to get him to come up here a day or two before but this time just couldn't get him. The first song in a broadcast is always a trial to me because I am so humbugged with my bronchial wheeziness that it is about all I can concentrate on for the first two minutes as the mike picks up every frog. But it did my heart good to have you say this was true Lieder singing—now I am getting a better idea all the time of when I can make a fuss of the words and when I must concentrate on line more etc. Quelle vie!

At this time there were many programmes to be planned, including one for her recital with Bruno Walter at the Edinburgh Festival of 1951. The following letter gave welcome guidance:

Dearest Kathleen,

Many thanks for your kind letter. Believe me that it gives me great joy to think forward to our reunion at Usher Hall.

As for our programme, I am writing you here a list of Brahms Lieder which in my opinion are all like composed especially for you:

> Liebestreu
> Oh wüsst ich doch den Weg zurück
> Geheimnis
> Wir Wandelten
> Auf dem Kirchhof
> Ständchen
> Nicht mehr zu dir zu gehen
> Wie bist du mein Königin
> Die Mainacht
> Auf dem See
> Dein blaues Auge
> Ruhe, Süssliebchen
> Oh brich nicht, Steg   (^{1}) Heimkehr Vol. I.

Of Mahler I think the following songs would be just what you could wish for:

> Wo die schönen Trompeten
> Ich ging mit Lust
> Ich atmet einen Linden Duft

---

[1] I am not sure of the exact words in this case. I think this Lied is in the 3rd volume, but you will easily find it. It is a very fiery song and might be a 'find' for you. As such a find I also consider 'Ruhe, Süssliebchen.'

Ich bin der Welt abhanden gekommen
Urlicht
Um Mitternacht.

These last three songs are of a religious character, and particularly
'Um Mitternacht' is one of the most powerful religious invocations,
marvellously suited to end a programme on a solemn and uplifting
note. We don't have to be afraid to include 'Urlicht' in the group
of Mahler songs. Although it is a part of the symphony, it is at the
same time a Lied which could stand on its own, and Mahler had
composed it before he wrote the symphony.

Of course you shall also sing Schubert, and if you have a particular
liking for some songs of Hugo Wolf, let me know them by all
means. 'Starke Einbildungskraft' is a song which could be understood only by a German-speaking public, and I cannot advise to
do it. I love Cornelius' Brautlieder, but I don't have the feeling that
they would appeal to a public like ours.

Dearest Kathleen, I want you to know that we think of you here
in great friendship, and Lotte and I send you our best love and
good wishes for a happy Christmas and New Year.

Always yours,

Bruno Walter.

Kathleen sent the following programme:

Schubert: *An die Leier*
Ganymed
Lachen und Weinen
Wanderers Nachtlied
Suleika 1 & 2

Mahler: *Wo die schönen Trompeten blasen*
Ich bin der Welt abhanden gekommen
Ich ging mit Lust
Ich atmet einen Linden Duft
Um Mitternacht

Brahms: *Liebestreu*
Ruhe, Süssliebchen
Auf dem See
Dein blaues Auge
Die Mainacht
Heimkehr

Both the Mahler and the Brahms songs were chosen entirely from those suggested by Bruno Walter.

His reply read:

Your programme seems excellent to me, and I am not afraid that it will impress the public as too much on the serious side. This could only affect the choice of the encores, and if, for instance, your first encore would be 'Du bist die Ruh', you easily can follow up with songs of a more graceful character.

It was my intention to do Mahler's 'Lied von der Erde' in March in New York. Do you think it possible to arrange your season accordingly? I am sure if you could accept the Philharmonic Symphony Society's invitation for that concert your management could surround it with a considerable number of other appearances which would make your voyage worth while.

With all good wishes for a happy New Year,

Most sincerely yours,

Bruno Walter.

On 18th November 1950 Kathleen and Gerald Moore set off together for Holland to give a series of recitals. Kathleen treasured the letter he wrote to her afterwards:

Kathleen darling,

I am sitting in the lounge where I have so often sat watching you sip your Bols, and I felt I must write a little love-letter to you to await your return.

The entire three weeks visit to Holland with you has been such undiluted pleasure: I have never felt so comfortable or happy in all my years with any other singer. On trips like this when two people are so constantly thrown together, it is very easy for little temperamental tiffs or moods or little misunderstandings to cause temporary clouds where personal relationships are concerned—but I venture to think that nothing like this has occurred with us. Certainly I have felt happy all the time—thanks entirely to your sweet nature, your unselfishness and un-prima donna-ishness! The only moment when I felt called on to exercise some authority as your male escort was that most regrettable incident when we supped at the Voûte's, and you nearly poured your soup into the wrong aperture!

I have said nothing of the pleasure—of the enormous pleasure that your thrilling triumph has given me. You have sung gloriously and it has been wonderful for me to be able to enjoy a share of this huge success. Thank you, my dear, for everything. May I have the luck to be associated with you for many years to come.

Bon voyage to you, and once again—all my thanks.

Your devoted friend,

Gerald.

The rest of Kathleen's work in 1950 was in the British Isles. For the first time for several years the Ferrier family were able to spend Christmas together. They were joined by Mrs. Tillett and a friend of hers from New Zealand, Bernadine Hammond, known to her friends as 'Bernie'. At the end of the day 'our father' made his customary remark—'Well, this has been the best Christmas I've ever had!'

A few days later he had a cold and retired reluctantly to bed. The doctor diagnosed influenza and when Kathleen had to leave for Holland on the 2nd January he was still not much better. Snow was falling heavily when she left the house. Win, who thought it unlikely that any plane would be able to take off, expected her to return home, but when some hours later the telephone rang, it was a call from Kathleen to say that she had arrived in Holland.

She wrote to Mrs. Tillett:

Dearest Emmie,

I don't mind the words of folk songs being printed—they like to have them when they're in another language—(I'm talking about Zurich!).

I've just rung Paddy and she says 'Bernie' called round to see Pop—how terribly kind of her—I *do* appreciate it. Paddy says he's a lot better the last two days so that's a relief.

The flight was all right after the take-off—though a young man in front lost all his Christmas cheer for the *whole* journey! But I'd had mi 'Kwells' and I tucked in—I was so glad to be up and on an even keel!

After the first night of *Orfeo* in Amsterdam Kathleen wrote to Win:

The first night was a wow and nothing awful happened and I quite enjoyed it. If I could act confidently, it's really much easier

than a recital, but I still feel it's a lot of playacting—where I live
and love and die in a song.

Joan Cross and Hans Schneider are coming on Saturday,
Roderick Jones tomorrow—and Otokar Kraus is already here, so
it's like home. Off to the Hague tonight for *Orfeo* and have just had
my hair ringletted for it—the whole dining room stares! I leave
here for Paris on the 17th.

From Paris she wrote to Mrs. Tillett:

I'm thrilled with my French lessons with Pierre Bernac—he
roared with mirth at first—but in the nicest way!—but now he's
getting quite excited—and even I, by a series of lip contractions
that might prove serious if indulged in too long!—can hear an
improvement! I should love a lesson a day for twelve months—
then I should feel I was really getting somewhere! I passed on your
message and he purred with pleasure. Why not pop over to Paris
for the week-end and hear my second concert???

and a week later:

Dearest Emmie,

I *KNEW* you wouldn't let me have all my own way with Pierre
Bernac!!! Oh! clever Emmie! T'will be lovely to see you in Paris.
Wish you could have been there for the recital—it *did* go well—
but I'll have to put my best foot forward for the 18th. (Programme
still not settled!)

All tickets and arrangements doing fine and managed to change
money, languages and trains twice from Paris to St. Gallen—and
still have five bags at the end of it. I think I'm a ruddy wizard!
What I would do if everybody didn't speak English, I can't think.

God bless, love, and see you soon.

Kaff.

'Our father', who was now 83 years old, seemed to be getting
slowly better. But suddenly he became very ill. When Kathleen
was on her way to Rome, it was clear that he would not live
long. Win sent a cable to await Kathleen in Rome, asking her
to telephone. When she did, Win had great difficulty in per-
suading her not to return. There was nothing to be gained by
it; her father was unconscious and could not live more than a
few hours. Win argued that her father would not wish Kathleen

to abandon her tour and undertake a long air journey in bad weather. Reluctantly and sadly she had to agree.

From Rome she wrote:

Dearest Win,

It was wonderful to speak to you this morning and hear you sounding so calm and managing everything so well. I am at a loss here and feel that I am not pulling my weight. I *do* hope I am doing the right thing in not coming home and that you don't feel I'm getting out of the responsibility.

I have two days off here to rehearse with a new pianist and never felt less like singing in my life. *Later:* Have only just got your second telegram—thank you love for sending it, also yours and Paddy's letters this morning. Rosalind and Alec [Maitland] send their fondest love—they were round here by 10 a.m. this morning to see if they could do anything. Poor old Pop! I shall miss him—but I think he enjoyed life, and especially being in Hampstead—don't you? I do hope the funeral arrangements are not too complicated and miserable—and don't hesitate to take taxis everywhere for comfort and convenience. And ask me for any more money—I'll do all the paying there is. How kind of Emmie to come up—bless her a thousand times! And how lovely that Pop had just had his best Christmas ever—and he really meant it!

Much love to you and bless you for everything. Can Paddy have a friend in? I don't like the thought of her there by herself. Look after yourself and I shall be thinking of you all the time. God bless. Love, Kath.

On the day of the funeral, she wrote:

Dearest Win,

Have been thinking of you all today and hoping that it was a lovely service (as I thought it was for Mr. Tillett)—and hoping you are not too weary and miserable with all the arrangements you would have to make. I *am* grateful to you, love, for coping so marvellously, and I *do* hope things were made as smooth as possible for you. I shall be thinking of you and Emmie tomorrow, finishing your paintings. I'm glad Mrs. Jewitt was a help—she's a calm person I should think in illness, she's had to deal with so much, and I do hope Uncle Bert came to give you moral support. I am grateful to whatever Gods there are for making such a peaceful ending for him, bless him. He was wonderful when you think—apart from anaemia he never had an illness in his life. It must have been abstinence and smoking too much!

Things go fairly well here—though my concert last night in Rome was only a third full to start—in a small hall (600)—I'd been told it was sold out. But it seems they're subscription tickets and if they don't know a name, they won't come. So I told the manager, if they didn't come, they'd never know a name! However, it filled up at the end, but they are the shuffliest audience I've ever known. It certainly isn't worth staggering around on my own, trying to cope with strange languages and monies, to sing to such people. I was in fairly good voice I think and they shouted 'Brava' and 'Bis'.

Then the manager came round afterwards with all the people there and asked me to change my programme for Milan—on the spot—so I let out all my inhibitions and repressions and went prima donna and waved my arms and said, 'Not bloody likely'—or words to that effect—and enjoyed myself. But when I thought about it afterwards, it was really my fault as I had mixed up the programmes—so it was temper—not temperament.

I have glowing notices this morning and I am told I have had a *succès fou*—but I still don't like 'em. I'm told they're much worse in Florence, so anything may happen in the *Kindertotenlieder* tomorrow. Was up at six this morning to catch train for here—no heat and enormously cold—and straight to rehearsal and no breakfast—but I'm all right.

The Maitlands have come with me and I think they will be terrified in case the audience shout or spit! They are darlings and have been absolute pets. And Alec's cousin—Catherine Henderson—has been an absolute angel, and put her car at my disposal and given me meals and been just adorable.

Rome is amazing and I'll bring you one day (*D.V.*) if only to see the Colosseum and the Pantheon—the latter built 2000 B.C.!! The pianist is very good, though he *will* duet with me in a hideous falsetto all the time—but he's a trier and very sensitive, so I can bear anything. I daren't leave anything about here—and I lock my fur coat up all the time—I had all my Swiss francs stolen the day I arrived, about £30, taken out of my bag, and however much you give a porter or taxi, they shout for more. This is one country I'll never retire to! But I'm getting good at shouting back and saying 'Basta, basta'—and often adding the 'rd'!

Am just going to have dinner with the Maitlands then go straight to bed. The concert is at 5 p.m. tomorrow of all awful times.

Hardly saw any snow in Switzerland—must have come another way!

Look after yourself, love, and much love and bless you for everything.

Do you need any money? Do say. Will write again soon.

My love—Kaff.

After a concert in Milan, a broadcast from Turin and a recital in Perugia, she took the train for Paris. As there were five free days before her next concert and she was alone, she spent a good deal of her time exploring Paris. She also had three more lessons with Pierre Bernac.

Later he wrote:

My English is too poor to allow me to express what I would like to say: my deep admiration for her 'conscience professionelle' as we say; the care and the scruple with which she approached each phrase, each word, each note. Without knowing French at all she succeeded to sing it really very well, not so well as her German of course, but she was beginning to master it wonderfully. We worked on several songs and mostly on Chausson: *Poème de l'Amour et de la Mer* which she sang finally like nobody else in the world and in the time. I still remember going through it in Edinburgh during the festival of 1951 on the piano of the Institut Français. Poulenc was playing. How thrilling it was for me to hear gradually the music and the poem being magnified by this glorious voice and this incomparable musicianship.

When her father had died, Win, knowing what a sad home-coming it would be for Kathleen, and being in need of a change herself, arranged to go with Mrs. Tillett to meet Kathleen in Paris. On the way they discussed the new situation. Without 'our father' Paddy would be alone a great deal, and in any case she was contemplating getting married. Kathleen needed some-one to look after her. Mrs. Tillett suggested that Bernie, who had spent Christmas Day with them, might be a possibility. Although she was a nurse and had looked after Mrs. Tillett's mother when she was ill, she was tired of nursing and anxious for a change. She was a good housekeeper and could also help with Kathleen's correspondence. Win, knowing that Kathleen liked Bernie, thought it might be an excellent idea.

On arrival at the hotel in Paris they found that Kathleen was out at a rehearsal. When she came in she flung herself into Win's arms with a most unusual show of emotion. Win assumed that their father's death and the recent unsatisfactory and lonely tour accounted for it.

At the concert on Sunday the 18th February 1951 in the Théâtre des Champs-Elysées Kathleen sang *Cara Sposa*, by Handel, Purcell's *Hark the Ech'ing Air*, *Che Faro* and the *Four Poems of St. Teresa*, by Lennox Berkeley. The Orchestre de la Société des Concerts du Conservatoire was conducted by Carl Schuricht. The audience took Kathleen to their hearts as soon as she came on to the platform and after the concert the artist's room was packed with enthusiastic people.

The week-end was delightful. They dined with a friend of Kathleen's and saw a wonderful collection of books, glass and china. They wandered along the quays in the February sunshine and sat outside a café sipping Pernod and watching the passers-by.

CHAPTER SIXTEEN

Orfeo

AN actor of world repute seldom has 'one day stands'; yet a singer of equal status rarely sings in the same place on two consecutive days. Most musicians have instruments to play, and although these may be affected by different conditions, yet the notes are not so influenced by the health and wellbeing of the performer as those of a singer, who indeed carries the whole weight of her career *in her own person*. In this respect Kathleen had a special responsibility. From 1948 onwards there was no other contralto in Europe doing work comparable either in variety or extent.

Between the beginning of January 1948 and March 1953 the time taken up with singing abroad amounted to seventeen months—eight in America and nine in Europe. On one tour in America there had been difficulties of travel and differences with the management. A later one however was described as the perfect tour. A visit to Europe had been memorable for the challenge of Salzburg; another for the supreme experience of the Bach Festival in Vienna; a third had been shadowed by the death of her father.

Both professionally and personally Kathleen was a 'lone she-wolf'. In such circumstances the support of a home is highly important. It is at once a place in which the roots of security can grow: a foundation and a springboard. Although much space has been given to her visits abroad, it should not be in doubt that Kathleen was devoted to her home, her family and close friends. It was in Britain that her major contribution to music was made. The present chapter gives some account of the times between her foreign tours and deals especially with the final period at home.

When she returned from America on the 10th February 1948 there were engagements planned for the following eight weeks, the first being a performance of *The Dream of Gerontius,* conducted by Sir Malcolm Sargent, in the Albert Hall. She sang in the same oratorio in Manchester with the Hallé Orchestra and in Bach's *St. John Passion,* in five performances of the *St. Matthew Passion,* in the *Mass in B Minor* and in *Messiah.* There were recitals in schools, music clubs, churches and halls, large and small. Sherborne, Oxford, Bristol Cathedral, Huddersfield. Her broadcasts included a recording for *Music in Miniature* and a performance of a work by Lennox Berkeley. He wrote: 'I only had (alas) one experience of working with Kathleen. This was when she broadcast the first performance of my *Four Poems of St. Teresa* for contralto and string orchestra. Apart from her great gifts and professional competence, of which it is unnecessary to speak, I was at once struck by her approach to the task. She put herself at the service of the music, seeking to enter into its spirit, rather than use it as a means for displaying her voice and talent. It is always the best artists who give one this impression, and with none have I felt it more strongly than with her. Coupled with this was an extraordinary understanding of what I was trying to express. There is no greater reward for a composer than to meet with such a response, and I shall always remember it with gratitude and affection.'

In the seven weeks following her return from Holland on the 3rd May 1948 there were performances of oratorio and many recitals, including a broadcast Thursday Concert, a *Lieder* recital in Wigmore Hall and a delightful Serenade Concert in the Orangery at Hampton Court.

At the Edinburgh Festival of 1948 she gave a recital in the Freemasons' Hall on the 26th August and sang in Bach's *Mass in B Minor* on the 29th. From there she went to the Three Choirs Festival, singing in the *St. Matthew Passion, The Dream of Gerontius, The Blessed Damozel* and *Messiah.*

After flying from Scandinavia on the 30th September there was a day's rest before beginning three months devoted to oratorios and recitals. By this time her name was becoming associated with Mahler's music and having sung *Kindertotenlieder* in a broadcast from the north, it was performed again in Manchester, Sheffield, Bradford, Edinburgh and London.

In 1949 much of the year was taken up with concerts in Europe and America, but during the few weeks when she was at home there were some memorable concerts—recitals in Belfast, Dublin and Cambridge, two performances of Brahms's *Four Serious Songs*, transcribed for orchestra by Sir Malcolm Sargent, one recital at the Edinburgh Festival and another in the Central Hall, Westminster, with Bruno Walter, and three performances of *Kindertotenlieder*, conducted by him.

Of many recitals, one given in the Central Hall, Westminster, with Benjamin Britten and Peter Pears, was undertaken to help the funds of the United Nations Association. All three artists stayed on the platform throughout the concert—the singers taking turn and turn about in singing a Handel aria or a Schubert Lied and joining for duets by Morley and Purcell—a most enjoyable concert, the forerunner of others on the same pattern.

In October 1950 Kathleen sang Brahms's *Alto Rhapsody* and *The Dream of Gerontius*, both conducted by Sir John Barbirolli. Since their first performance together two years previously, collaboration with him had given her ever increasing joy. His passionate absorption in music, his meticulous attention to detail, his insistence on adequate rehearsals and a high standard of performance filled her with admiration.

Personally too, they had much in common: a love of good food, a sense of humour, a love of home and homeliness, an impatience with pretentiousness. As they came to know one another better she found in him an attitude towards music similar to her own—critical, questing, accepting nothing on trust, striving always for perfection: someone indeed who not only spoke her own language, but also from whom she could learn.

Having at his suggestion studied Chausson's *Poème de l'Amour et de la Mer* she sang it for the first time in Manchester on the 28th February 1951 with the Hallé Orchestra, conducted by Sir John. In the next three years she sang with him almost all the works dearest to her, and under his influence her interpretative powers grew.

Travelling the length and breadth of the British Isles, she appeared personally in more than two hundred and fifty different places—villages, towns and cities; and to some of them she returned several times. There were concerts with amateur music makers. Alan Kirby, Founder and Musical Director of the Croydon Philharmonic Society, wrote:

Kathleen devoted a great deal of time to singing at amateur choral concerts that ranged from the large scale performances of famous choirs to those of the smaller, but no less important, ones in provincial towns. It mattered not to Kathleen if she were singing one of the familiar works in the choral repertoire, such as *Messiah* or *Elijah*, or one of the lesser known, such as *The Kingdom* or *The Apostles*, her attitude to the programme never varied. You were not made to feel you were being favoured by the visit of a great singer, but Kathleen gave the impression that she had come to help in making a worth while performance. She never 'made an entry' to a rehearsal, but just slipped into her seat as unobtrusively as possible.

Her vivid powers of interpretation were not made the vehicle of theatrical display or used to focus the limelight on the performer. Her fine musicianship—she knew everybody else's part as well as her own—was never forced into prominence, but was there to be brought to the aid of all those with whom she came in contact.

No performance was ever a perfunctory one for Kathleen, she always gave of her best, and by doing so inspired others to greater heights.

This was her attitude to her work on the concert platform, and one might imagine from it that she was a serious-minded girl in all she did, but nothing could be further from the truth. If you met her on a social occasion you would not guess that she was one of the world's great singers.

Before she flew to Cologne on the 15th March, 1951, Kathleen asked Bernie to arrange for her to see a doctor on her return. Having sung in Germany and Holland, she went to Lewes for a performance of the *St. Matthew Passion* on Good Friday, 23rd March, and the following day had a medical examination. There was a lump in her breast which the doctor said must be removed as soon as possible. All work for the next few months was immediately cancelled.

A fortnight after her operation Kathleen was looking well and had regained her high spirits. Friends who came prepared to sympathise found her as gay and lively as ever. If she was distressed by the effects of the operation, she did not show it and indeed seemed to have accepted the situation and come to terms with it. Perhaps there was relief in the knowledge that what for so long she had secretly dreaded had now happened—and been overcome. There was the same exhilaration as that felt after a bad air raid, when she had written, 'Still here!' Only once did she speak seriously about it. 'I worried a bit beforehand in case I should not be brave enough.'

On her 39th birthday, 22nd April, she sat up in bed, receiving and entertaining many callers who arrived with gifts. As they sat round her bed laughing and talking, one of them said: 'I like this club! I think I shall join it!'

The nurses also became members, bringing in supplies of tea at frequent intervals! Dame Myra Hess sent champagne and oysters—a contribution to the birthday dinner which was much appreciated. As the last visitor reluctantly left Kathleen remarked: 'This is the loveliest birthday I've ever had!'

The doctors had advised deep ray therapy on the breast and spine ' . . . to make sure', Kathleen said, 'that I shall have no further trouble.' Before her first treatment the sister warned her that it might make her feel ill for a while. Afterwards Kathleen said: 'I thought I would show her that it wouldn't get *me* down.' She grumbled only because until the course of about six weeks' treatment was finished she was not allowed to have a bath.

Soon after coming out of hospital she was having lunch with some friends at Casa Prada. There was so much laughter that everybody in the room turned round to see what was happening. Kathleen had opened the back of a locket she wore and emptied on to the palm of her hand some black spidery fragments, asking her friends to guess what they were. No one could guess. 'They're mi stitches', she said. 'When sister took them out I asked her if I could have them. Much more interesting than a lock of hair!'

As well as adjusting herself to the effects of the operation, Kathleen had to get used to the gap caused by her father's death.

The room which had been his was made into a music room and Kathleen began to look for a grand piano to take the place of the one won in 1928 and which was now past its prime. At that time good pianos were difficult to find, and Dame Myra Hess, when she heard of Kathleen's need, offered to lend her one which she was not using. This piano, beautiful in tone and appearance, gave great pleasure.

The little room next to the kitchen was turned into a dining room. There were some riotous parties in it, often with twelve or more people squeezed around the table. The meals were never elaborate but there was always wine. Kathleen loved to play the hostess and although she always felt responsible for keeping the party going, she liked to sit back, having encouraged other people to 'do their party piece.'

At the end of May, being now well enough to go on holiday, she and Bernie went to stay at Alfriston in Sussex. Bernie wrote:

Kath was in great form, walking for miles over the Downs and breathing deeply the good Sussex air. At this time painting and photography were her chief interests; she was also learning a group of Brahms songs for the forthcoming Edinburgh Festival. This was done mornings and evenings, sitting up in bed.

The evenings were hilariously funny. A friend had driven us down to Sussex and left his rather dilapidated black and white sports cap. Every night Kath would put this on at a most saucy angle and sit up in bed in dainty night attire learning her songs.

One of the first sketches we did in Sussex was of the little church surrounded by trees in Alfriston. To get the best view we had to put the easels up on a slope and then stand astride and paint, as it were, uphill. It was heavenly weather and Kath hummed her songs as she painted—at that time *Nell* by Fauré was on her mind. One day a bus-load of people arrived to disturb the peace, and I heard someone say, 'Look, a real live artist.'

Kath could achieve in a short time the general effect of the subject. She worked quickly but carefully. When I was in trouble, in fact in despair, Kath would say, 'Just slap a bit of paint on love, it's only fun anyway!' She only became ruffled when on some of the hot days the flies fell into the paint and 'committed suicide'.

At night, having trailed home with our wet masterpieces we went straight upstairs. The paintings were hung on the oak beams by sticking drawing pins through them. Then the praising and the criticism began. From a comfortable position on her bed, Kath would occasionally leap up and add a cloud to the sky or alter a line or a curve which she said made all the difference.

From Alfriston she paid her first visit to Gerald and Enid Moore's lovely home on Box Hill. During this visit Gerald took us out in his car, and while he was buying some cigarettes, Kath, who had not driven for years, slid into the driver's seat and drove the car down the road. She chuckled at the thought of what Gerald's face would look like when he found his car gone.

Before her illness Kathleen's last performance had been in Bach's *St. Matthew Passion*. For her return she chose Bach's *Mass in B Minor* conducted by Dr. Jacques in the Royal Albert Hall on 19th June 1951. At the rehearsal she received a rapturous welcome from the Bach Choir and Orchestra and after the performance *The Times* critic wrote of: 'Miss Kathleen Ferrier whose return from sickness could be a matter for general gratitude and rejoicing; her vocal and interpretative powers were unimpaired.'

On 1st July Kathleen went off to Holland for some performances of *Orfeo,* taking Bernie with her. As the plane taxied to a standstill at Schipol airport, Peter Diamand came forward with a bouquet of red roses and the cameras began to click. Kathleen wanted to see the newsreel which included this arrival, but she was too busy, so Bernie went. Just as the newsreel began, some people stood up to let others in, and by the time they sat down the incident was over. Bernie had to sit through the whole programme again, in order to see the part of the film showing their arrival: it lasted about thirty seconds.

Kathleen returned from Holland feeling very tired: the weather had been hot and oppressive; performing had tried her strength. A recital with Bruno Walter and a performance of Chausson's *Poème de l'Amour et de la Mer* with Sir John Barbirolli were planned for the Edinburgh Festival at the beginning of September, and she was anxious to have a really good rest until then. This proved difficult: there were many people who had been disappointed when her previous engagements had been cancelled and were clamouring for her services.

Apart from a few engagements which she felt obliged to fulfil and a weekly visit to hospital, she was free to enjoy a peaceful summer, to see her friends and go out into the country. There was a short holiday, staying with Sir John and Lady Barbirolli at Seaford which was enjoyable, not only for their companionship and affection, but for the pleasure of being with a family bound together by a strong feeling of unity. Kathleen, recently deprived of a devoted father and left with few close relatives, found it warmed her heart to be with this family, which included Sir John's nephew and niece, his mother, sister and brother.

A weekly feature of this period was the Sunday morning painting session. Kathleen, Bernie and Win joined Mrs. Tillett at her home in St. John's Wood, painting in the garden when the weather was warm enough and otherwise indoors. Often they painted the same still life group, but the results were different. There was much fun and laughter and occasional groans of despair, as the work proceeded. Kathleen always finished first and rested until the others were ready to stop. The session ended with lunch. One Sunday as Kathleen sat with a plate in front of her piled high with delicious food, she looked around at the others and said, 'Well, to look at me now, nobody would believe that I was "proper poorly".' A diary entry about this time reads: 'Went to Rye and Winchelsea— feeling like death.'

On the last day of August 1951, Kathleen travelled once more to the Edinburgh Festival, staying with the Maitlands. There followed a recital with Bruno Walter, which was broadcast, and a performance of Chausson's *Poème de l'Amour et de la Mer,* with Sir John Barbirolli. The music critic of *The Scotsman* said:

It is beautiful music, richly scored with an imaginative grasp of the possibilities inherent in the words. Certainly it was introduced under the best auspices on Friday night, for Kathleen Ferrier was the soloist. It is sometimes argued that her voice in all its splendour has a quality of reassurance that prevents her from expressing the full measure of pain or suffering, but on Friday her treatment of the latter part of *La Mort de l'Amour* was sufficient answer.

After Edinburgh there was a fairly full programme of concerts up and down the country. On the 2nd October there was a broadcast from Manchester of *The Enchantress* which Sir Arthur Bliss had written for her. He wrote:

It was not until 1951 that I first met Kathleen Ferrier, although I had heard her beautiful voice many times before then, both on the radio and on records. My opportunity came when, in admiration of her singing, I wrote a special 'scena' that she could sing with an orchestra at concerts.

I well remember the autumn morning when I climbed to her home in Frognal to rehearse my music with her. I can vividly recall her welcoming smile and charming hospitality, the talk about the pictures she was painting, her quiet music-room, and the first run-through at the piano.

She sat beside me humming her part, and occasionally striking a note on the piano. She asked me to describe her role in this dramatic 'scena', and I told her she was a proud Syracusan lady, deserted by her lover, and now invoking the powers of black magic to win him back. The words came from the Second Idyll of Theocritus, and had been translated for me by Henry Reed.

As I went through the score with her I could not help feeling that though the solo part did some justice to the magnificent two octaves of her voice, Kathleen herself bore no resemblance to this Medea-like heroine, needing a nobler role for *her* personality.

In October of that year, 1951, I went to Manchester to hear her give a broadcast of *The Enchantress*. We lunched together near the Art Gallery, and afterwards visited it to see an exhibition of modern English painting. She was in a gay and happy mood, and I remember teasing her about her old fashioned ideas of painting, and trying to convince her that her true leanings were towards purely abstract art.

One of the unforgettable things about Kathleen was her ability to enjoy the moment. She had a completely easy and natural manner when meeting new admirers of her gift. The balance between pride and modesty that she showed in talking about herself is found, I believe, in all great artists.

The same evening, at a party after the concert, I saw another side of her, for she sang to us almost in a rapt trance, unaccompanied folk songs.

Her personality on the concert platform expressed a radiant happiness. She had a glorious gift, and she used it generously to the delight of millions.

AGED 39

Photo : Vogue

WITH GERALD MOORE

WITH PETER PEARS AND BENJAMIN BRITTEN

Photo: Paul Shillabeer

EDINBURGH, 1952

In November the rebuilt Free Trade Hall in Manchester was to be opened. About this Sir John Barbirolli wrote:[1]

> After much thought I had what proved to be a real inspiration. Since this was a great Lancashire occasion, what could be more fitting than to have the most exquisite and resplendent Rose of Lancaster—our Katie—as soloist in Elgar's *Land of Hope and Glory*? By some alchemy of sincerity and inborn genius, she made the rather outmoded words seem not in the least incongruous, and lifted the whole thing to a noble climax, which moved everyone, not least the conductor, to tears.

This day was memorable for Kathleen too, and so was the week-end following it, when the Barbirollis took her for drives in Cheshire. In the following few weeks she had no concert engagements and revelled in her freedom to go out to lunch or dinner, attend a matinee, see a performance of *Turandot* and *Billy Budd* at Covent Garden, and play the piano for pleasure.

At Christmas time she went to many parties and New Year's Eve was spent with her friends Jamie and Yvonne Hamilton. In *The Times* Alan Pryce-Jones wrote:

> No conventional tribute can reflect the glow of Kathleen Ferrier's personality. Those who were there will not forget a dinner party on the New Year's Eve of 1952, in the house of Mrs. Hamish Hamilton. After dinner on an impulse Kathleen decided to sing— first 'Ich grolle nicht' and 'Du holde Kunst' and 'Gretchen am Spinnrade'. But there was nothing tragic about her view of the world; it was above all warm and gay. And before long she was singing absurdities of all kinds, little parodies and inventions, and then folk-songs. At last, suddenly, at the stroke of midnight, she fell serious again, and that peaceful heartening voice brought in a new year with the hope and courage which anyone who knew her recognised as unconquerable.

This was one of many gay evenings spent with the Hamiltons. As well as parties at their house and at hers, there were visits to theatres—to the Old Vic and Sadlers Wells. Jamie Hamilton took her dancing on several occasions and found her wonderfully light and smooth. To his surprise, she knew all the tunes and hummed them while they danced.

[1] *Kathleen Ferrier: A Memoir.* Hamish Hamilton.

At the beginning of 1952 she wrote to an American friend, Mrs. Cress:

> We have had a grand time. Bernie, Win and I went to Mrs. Tillett's on Christmas Day—opened presents and painted a pheasant, as being in the Christmas spirit. One of the best Christmasses I remember.
> I start again on the 7th January with the *Four Serious Songs* in the Albert Hall with Sir Malcolm Sargent conducting—and from then on I am very busy. But I have had a good long rest and it has been heavenly to be at home for so long.
> Sir John Barbirolli came up the other night and brought his 'cello, and we went through several sonatas and pieces and had a wonderful time. I adore accompanying and he loves playing, so we were very pleased with ourselves.

At home in the winter Kathleen loved to pile up a roaring fire and sit with the cat on her lap listening to the radio, doing a crossword puzzle or reading a book. She also enjoyed playing Canasta. At this time she offered thanks for her blessings, taking the utmost pleasure, like her father before her, in the little happenings of every day. Although she went to hospital about once a month for a check up, her spirit and vitality remained unimpaired and she achieved a happiness unshadowed, as far as anyone could tell, by the possibility of any further developments. Realising clearly what the future might have in store, she accepted the situation, as she had always done, without self pity or resentment and with a heightened realisation of all that life had to offer.

Kathleen's first engagement in 1952 was at the Winter Promenade Concerts, when she sang Brahms's *Four Serious Songs* in the transcription by Sir Malcolm Sargent. A week later there was an engagement to sing Chausson's *Poème de l'Amour et de la Mer* with the London Symphony Orchestra, conducted by Gaston Poulet. At the rehearsal in the morning it was found that the wrong parts had been sent from Paris. This time, unlike her first Promenade Concert, it was impossible to get the parts in time. The rest of the story was told in the *Daily Mail*:

> If we were disappointed in not being able to hear Kathleen Ferrier sing Chausson's *Poème de l'Amour et de la Mer* with orchestral accompaniment, we had the unexpected delight of hearing

Gerald Moore demonstrate how marvellous it can sound in the black and white of the piano. No wonder Miss Ferrier kissed his hand and he hers.

After this, to help the funds of the English Opera Group, Kathleen sang in a series of concerts with Benjamin Britten and Peter Pears, in Nottingham, Birmingham, Manchester, Bristol, Liverpool and at the Victoria and Albert Museum in London. The programmes included two of Morley's canzonets, some Lieder, the *Dialogue of Coridon and Mopsa*, from Purcell's *The Fairy Queen*, some folk songs and a Canticle—*Abraham and Isaac*—specially written for Peter Pears and Kathleen by Benjamin Britten. Kathleen could well imagine Isaac's feelings of resignation.

It was during one of these concerts that, when walking off the platform, she appeared to trip and wrench her back. After this she was in some pain, although the audience was not aware of it, and feeling the need for some help, she telephoned for Bernie, who wrote:

The weather was severe: Kathleen's condition made her particularly sensitive to cold and draughts. I remember finding her in bed, fully clothed, with all her coats on top of her, shivering with cold. She could not bear to get out of bed to put another shilling in the gas meter. At another hotel there was central heating in the hall and passages but not in the bedrooms. In her room there was a fireplace which had the look of never having been used. Kath asked the porter to light a fire in her room. The porter looked rather blank, but in a few minutes he arrived with the necessary wood. After half-an-hour of a smoke-filled room the fire was blazing and the fender was full of coal and wood. Every time Kath woke up in the night she stoked it up and by morning she was at last warm. Before leaving next morning, she built up a colossal fire, so that the girls who came to tidy the room would be warm.

To Mrs. Cress she wrote:

28th January, 1952.

I have just done my first work since Edinburgh, nine recitals in two weeks and I have weathered the storm well.

For some concerts I have been with Gerald Moore who is an angel and Benjamin Britten and Peter Pears for others. They've all gone well and I have been spoiled to death by them. Now I'm almost home again. Look after yourself and don't worry about those extra pounds as long as you are well—that's what matters!

On the 7th February she flew to Belfast for a recital with Gerald Moore at Queens University. King George VI had died the previous day, and while in Belfast she was asked by telephone to take part in the broadcast Memorial Concert, singing part of *The Dream of Gerontius,* conducted by Sir Malcolm Sargent.

After this she went to hospital for an X-ray examination of her back. A projected tour in Switzerland and Germany was cancelled when the report came through that more treatment was necessary. For a time she visited hospital three times a week. Sometimes afterwards she suffered from discomfort and nausea and had to go to bed for a few hours, but still contrived to see her friends and to go to concerts and theatres.

19th February, 1952.

It is lovely to be at home, and I have been taking life easily and very lazily—staying in bed in the morning—napping in the afternoon, and several times going gay at night, which has been a nice change for me. Haven't sung a note for ages but have been playing chamber music with a friend of Myra Hess and with Barbirolli and his wife—they are 'cello and oboe respectively, and I play the piano. I love accompanying but ordinarily don't have much time.

I go to the hospital at intervals so that they can keep an eye on me, and apart from rheumatiz in my back, feel okeydoke.

I start working again on the 25th March, so have a little time to idle. I'm very lazy at heart!

At the end of March she felt well enough to work again and sang at several concerts. As she walked on to the platform of the Albert Hall to sing the *St. Matthew Passion,* Win thought her movements appeared stiff, but afterwards Kathleen said, 'It was only a bit of my old rheumatiz.' She was determined, whatever happened, to go ten days later to Manchester to sing *Gerontius* and *Messiah,* because they were to be conducted by Barbirolli. Bernie went with her.

By this time Win had become deeply concerned about Kathleen's health. Having been told that, after an operation such as

Kathleen had undergone, it was common for 'secondaries' to occur for several months afterwards, she had gone on hoping that they would cease. It was now a year since the operation and there was still no improvement. Something more must obviously be done. Feeling that Kathleen's optimistic attitude was her greatest ally in combating the disease and knowing what faith she had in the doctors who were treating her, it was difficult to know the best course to take. Yet nothing must be left undone which offered any possibility of a cure. On returning from Manchester Bernie told Win that Sir John had also been much concerned about the pain Kathleen was having in her back.

It was decided to ask him if he would try to persuade her to see another specialist. When Win telephoned him he gladly agreed. Unfortunately, before he arrived Bernie accidentally mentioned the matter. Kathleen was furious. She was afraid —quite mistakenly—that if she asked for a second opinion her doctors might refuse to continue treating her. Probably she was disturbed too at having her own misgivings confirmed. In due course, however, she did see a famous specialist. He told her that she could not have better attention than she was getting. He also said that he had never known anyone able to do so much work while having such treatment and that, if it became necessary, there was another line of defence. This was reassuring.

Kathleen went once again to Manchester to sing in three performances of *Das Lied von der Erde,* one of them broadcast. As usual she stayed with the Barbirollis and on her birthday she wrote in her diary: 'Heavenly birthday party mit cake!' There was another occasion a week later which gave her great pleasure. She was asked to sing at a private party at which Queen Elizabeth, the Queen Mother, and Princess Margaret were to be present. Many of her friends were going and Gerald Moore was playing for her. 'Party marvellous', she wrote. 'Sang and sang. Princess Margaret sang too. Memorable evening.'

On the 13th May 1952 Kathleen flew to Vienna to make a recording of *Das Lied von der Erde* with Bruno Walter. Bernie, who went with her, wrote:

> This was something Kath felt she must do, and although Vienna seemed a long way, she went off happily. We flew there in four

hours and were met by good friends at the airport. There followed a rather hair-raising journey through the Russian zone. Kath's only comment was, 'I wonder what the salt mines are really like!' We hoped that we would not find out. The days that followed were very hard and exacting, but Kath accepted all difficulties as a challenge, and with that attitude she rose above them. Hour after hour there were repeats, but she remained patient, how I don't know, for she was tired and often in discomfort. However, at the end of the day a good meal always seemed to revive her, and so it went on from day to day, till all was ready for the final recording.

Victor Olof wrote:

The recording of *Das Lied von der Erde* was the most moving experience and there is no doubt, if there is anything at all in the word inspiration, that this recording was definitely inspired. The feeling between Bruno Walter and Kathleen was always a very close one artistically and it was particularly so on this occasion. Bruno Walter said to me that this recording had to be made. And I think we all had a premonition of the future tragedy. You can imagine how furious I was when some stupid critic wrote that 'it is a pity that the celeste notes in the last few bars were not clear'. As if Dr. Bruno Walter and I had not realised this mistake. But the celeste being an instrument that is very unreliable with regard to touch and pianissimo we decided that the performance of Kathleen was so inspired that we simply could not be bothered with such trivialities.

As far as I am concerned her recording career hardly started. One must only be thankful that we have got as many records as we have.

To Mrs. Cress Kathleen wrote:

8th June, 1952.

I am feeling heaps better this month with the warmer weather and the doctor's very pleased mit mir. But for twelve months at least I shan't be leaving this country, so that if I need more treatment I shall be on the spot. It's not the singing that's wearying, it's the travelling and social side, and I'm doing so well that it seems potty to overdo, eh? So I shall work gently here and give a little less to the government!

Have just made another L.P. record—folk songs on one side— on the other Roger Quilter songs and arrangements of *Drink to me Only—Ye Banks and Braes!* etc. Hope you approve.

Much time that summer was spent in the little garden where in the spring she had put in seeds and plants. Instead of her usual Musician's Diary, she had a Gardener's which contained over a hundred pages of information and advice.

About the middle of July she and Bernie went to stay for a week-end with Burnet Pavitt in Hertfordshire. 'While we were there', wrote Bernie, 'we heard that the Queen was coming to stay with her uncle who lived in the next house. Kath's first comment when she was asked to sing for her was, "I'm sure she would rather sit with her feet up than listen to me singing!" However, it was finally arranged that Kath should sing the following evening at ten o'clock. There was a frantic rush back to London for suitable clothes and music. One of those rare and glorious summer days followed, and we spent most of it sitting in the sun. Kathleen seemed inspired to dance, pirouetting round the lawn on her bare feet, much to the amusement and delight of her friends. That afternoon the Royal Standard was hoisted into sight over the garden wall and it looked just wonderful.

'By the evening Kath was looking dignified and lovely in a black velvet frock. It was all so overwhelming that details are difficult to remember, but one picture stands out in my mind—Her Majesty sitting on a couch talking to Kath, who looked happy and quite at ease.'

Diary entry: 'Sang with Burnet accompanying. Chatted with the Queen for half an hour—lovely. Celebrated in champagne afterwards and played piano duets until 2.30 a.m.'

What she did not record was that after the duets her impersonation of herself, aged 18, playing a Beethoven sonata *con espressione* for an Academy examination was a side-splitting piece of clowning. Nor did she know that Her Majesty was aware of the true nature of her illness and had characteristically expressed concern.

During the summer Sir John Barbirolli talked to Kathleen about his great wish for her to sing *Orfeo* at Covent Garden.

When it was arranged, she spent happy hours rehearsing with him and between them they practically re-translated the whole work. Previously Kathleen had always sung it in Italian. When she began learning it in English, she found that first thing in the morning was the best time, so until she had learnt by heart a certain number of pages, she would not have her breakfast. Then she would sit back enjoying it and reading the morning paper.

Kathleen was in good form for the Edinburgh Festival of 1952. There was *Das Lied von der Erde* with van Beinum and the Concertgebouw Orchestra and a delightful performance, which was broadcast, of the Brahms *Liebeslieder Waltzes*, with Irmgard Seefried, Julius Patzak and Horst Günter.

Then followed a performance of *The Dream of Gerontius* conducted by Barbirolli on the 5th September and one of the *Messiah* the following day. So beautiful, Kathleen said, was this performance that it gave her one of her greatest experiences of her life.

On 7th October 1952 Kathleen made records of *O Thou that tellest, He was despised, Father of Heaven* and *Return O God of Hosts.* The following day *Grief for Sin, Qui sedes, Agnus Dei* and *All is Fulfilled.*

Of this occasion, Sir Adrian Boult wrote:

> Most memorable of all was the day we recorded for Decca four Handel and four Bach arias. I believe this was her last recording. The memory of our work together that day is very precious, and I only wish I had more to tell because it would mean enrichment of my own experience as a musician; working with her always was. Not only that, but of human experience too, because I can fully corroborate what has been far better said by many people— that any kind of personal contact with her was something to remember—something stimulating and inspiring.

On the 23rd October 1952 she flew to Dublin to sing *Gerontius* with Sir John Barbirolli, who was to receive the

honorary degree of Doctor of Music. The following speech was
retold by Kathleen in a strong Irish accent:

> When a truly great man visits us, it is the duty of every good
> Irishman to find out if such a personage has any Irish connections.
> You will be glad to learn that I have discovered that a definite
> link exists between Sir John and this country.
>
> During the 1914–1918 war, seventeen-year-old John Barbirolli
> volunteered for service and became a private in the Suffolk regiment.
> Over him was a sergeant-major who either sensed something Irish
> about this new recruit or experienced some difficulty in pronouncing
> the name properly. Thereupon Barbirolli was re-christened Bob
> O'Reilly. I think you will agree that the name of Bob O'Reilly
> places a man well within the four shores of Ireland.

On the 4th November Kathleen gave a recital in the Royal
Festival Hall and three weeks later a performance of *Das Lied von
der Erde,* conducted by Joseph Krips. Later he wrote: 'When
she sang the *Abschied* on the 23rd November 1952, we all, the
orchestra, the audience and myself, were in tears.'

On the 11th December, when she gave a recital in Carlisle,
there was a party afterwards, attended by many of her Cumberland friends. Jack Hetherington made a speech. 'The most
delightful thing about Kathleen', he said, 'is that although she
has become famous, success has not changed her. She is in fact
the same old Kath.' 'Not so much of the "old"', replied
Kathleen. Of this visit Bernie wrote: 'When we were in Carlisle
I noticed Kath limping rather badly. When I asked her about
it she said that she had not mentioned it before because to go
to London for treatment would have meant disappointing people
who had bought tickets for the concert. "Why did it have to
start again *now*, just when I am going to do *Orfeo*", she said.
"But it won't stop me, no matter what happens."'

On the 1st December a letter from Downing Street arrived,
causing great excitement. It contained news which had to be kept
secret for the time being. On New Year's Eve Kathleen, Bernie
and Win joined the Barbirolli family and as the clock struck
midnight, Sir John rose to make a speech. 'Dearest Commander,' he began. It was to congratulate Kathleen on having
been awarded a C.B.E.

About this time she wrote to Mrs. Cress:

> I am still rheumaticky from the neck down—so am staying quietly by the fire and going to bed in the afternoons like an old lady! But I'm happy as a lark.

In the new year, wrote Bernie, Kath began going to piano rehearsals at Covent Garden practically every day. The rehearsals were held in the foyer. The two other soloists arrived and the opera began to develop. From an outsider's point of view, watching this was very thrilling, though I was painfully aware of all the work that was going on. The foyer was measured out in proportion to the stage, and one of the girls—from the ballet I think—led Kath round and gave her a general idea of where she was to stand. Then the morning came when all rehearsals were on the stage. The huge curtain was down and the stage was alive with people all doing their various jobs. The first rehearsals were ballet; Kath was absolutely fascinated by one of the girls—Beriosova—who was perfectly lovely. Kath pointed to her own feet encased in snow-boots and said, 'Fancy me putting my big feet in amongst those girls.' Her one complaint was that she did not know where to put her feet.

Rehearsals usually started at 10 a.m. Kath stayed in bed at home till the last moment and then the struggle began. Once dressed she then had to get down very steep steps and over frosty slippery concrete and into a car. Pain in her legs and back made this very difficult for her. At the other end the struggle was the same, and I am thankful it was not seen by people other than Sir John, for it would have broken their hearts. Sometimes Sir John came home with her, but he felt as I did that to appear at all upset was letting Kath down. However, as soon as she got on the stage an amazing thing happened—I found it always very hard to believe—she was able to move about as if she had never in her life had a pain or an ache.

In January 1953 came a letter which gave Kathleen great pleasure. It was from Bernard Berenson whom she had met in Florence and whose collection of works of art she had been taken to see. He wrote: 'You made during the so short call an impression so indelible that ever since I have been longing to see you again. We hear you as often as the wireless waves bring us your moving voice. What would I not give to hear you as Orpheus.'

Of the first performance of *Orfeo* on the 3rd February 1953, Neville Cardus wrote: 'Seldom has Covent Garden Opera House been so beautifully solemnised as when Kathleen Ferrier flooded the place with tone which seemed as though classic shapes in marble were changing to melody, warm, rich-throated, but chaste.'

There were comments on her radiant presence, grace and dignity and the lack of artifice in her performance, but the notice which most delighted her, written by Richard Buckle in *The Observer* read:

> And none of the dancers moved with more expressive simplicity than Kathleen Ferrier, whose physical as well as vocal impersonation of Apollo's child is something I shall long remember.

'I think I shall take up Ballet next!' she remarked, on reading this.

At the second performance on the 6th February all went well until half way through the second act. Then Kathleen took a step forward and her leg appeared to give way under her. Continuing to play her part, she took advantage of the support of a balustrade and sang *Che Faro*. After some time the pain became unbearable and, leaning on Euridice's arm she walked slowly to the side of the stage and sat down in the wings. The orchestra continued playing and as she sat there the introduction to her last aria began. Walking on slowly and with great dignity she began to sing it without a tremor in her voice, and the opera finished, with many people unconscious that anything untoward had happened.

After she had stood for some time acknowledging the tumultuous applause, the curtain finally came down, and she was carried to her dressing room.

Her closest friends realised what she must have been suffering, but when they hurried anxiously round to her room, she was sitting smilingly receiving the people who had come to congratulate her.

When the last visitor had gone, Win said to her, 'What can I do for you, love?' She replied, 'Get me a stretcher.'

CHAPTER SEVENTEEN

Hear Her Sing

THERE was no understudy for the role of *Orfeo* (nor could there be, as Sir John said at the time), so the remaining two performances were cancelled, as also were all engagements for the following two or three months.

After X-ray photographs had been taken, it was found that a further course of treatment was necessary and arrangements were made for Kathleen to go into hospital once more.

In a few days she was happily settled there with everything organised to her liking. Sister Philips, who had looked after her before, was in charge again; the nurses were 'spoiling her to death', as she put it. The room was overflowing with flowers and on the window sill behind a curtain was an array of bottles which provided drinks for friends who called in the evening.

It was a disappointment that she was unable to attend the Investiture at Buckingham Palace on the 17th February 1953 to receive her C.B.E., but she was assured that an invitation to another one during the summer would be sent. Sir Benjamin Ormerod brought her a length of ribbon in the C.B.E. colours and this was pinned to her pillow.

During the last year there had been several invitations which for one reason or another she had been obliged regretfully to refuse: to sing at La Scala under Toscanini; to take the part of Brangäne in *Tristan and Isolde* at the Beyreuth Festival, to record the Bach *Mass in B Minor* with von Karajan. Now came another:

12th February, 1953.

Dear Miss Ferrier,
    We are now able to tell you that a fourth Casals Festival will take place at Prades this summer between the dates of 14th June

and 7th July. There will be five orchestral concerts with soloists and five concerts of chamber music. The composers represented will be Bach, Beethoven, Mozart and Schubert.

Mr. Casals would be very happy to invite you if you could arrange to come. We would have to know immediately, of course, so we could arrange the programme accordingly, and we could then correspond with you which work would be mutually agreeable.

We look forward to an early reply.

Most cordially yours,

Thea Dispeker
for the Music Committee:

Rudolf Serkin
Mieczyslaw Horszowski
Leopold Mannes

P.S. All my love to you!

to which she replied:

2nd March, 1953.

Dear Miss Dispeker,

Thank you so much for your letter of the 12th February. It was good to hear from you in a letter containing such a wonderful invitation.

I would have answered you before, but I damaged my leg in the middle of a performance of 'Orpheus' at Covent Garden, and am now in hospital and will probably be here for another month.

I am very much afraid I shall be unable to attend the Prades Festival, as I have already promised at that time to go to the festival in Rhodesia with the Hallé Society, and it would not be possible to manage both. I am bitterly disappointed, as I have heard such lovely accounts of the Festival from Dame Myra Hess, and can only hope that another year I may have this great privilege and pleasure.

With best wishes to you

Yours sincerely,

Kathleen Ferrier.

From John Newmark came the following:

Montreal.   29th March, 1952.

Dearest Kaff,

May I congratulate you right on the spot on the Grand Prix du Disque 1951[1] which according to the Paris weekly *Opera* of 5th March, was given to 'our' recording of Schumann and Brahms. Maybe you have not heard about it yet and I am the first to tell you, which would please me even more! You can imagine how proud I am and the whole town here is proud with me.

The doctors thought that six or seven weeks' treatment would be required before Kathleen could go home and when she did, it would be impossible for her to climb the steps to her flat. A ground floor flat or one possessing a lift would have to be found. Bernie and Win spent depressing days searching.

At last, in Hamilton Terrace, Bernie saw an empty maisonette. The sitting room looked out over a big garden and there was a room communicating with it which had wide French doors leading into the garden and would be suitable for Kathleen's bedroom. There was even a bathroom on the same floor.

When it was described to Kathleen she agreed to take it. She mentioned to Sister Philips her longing to see it so that she could plan the decorations and furnishing, and was told that it might be possible.

Accordingly, a few days later Kathleen in a wheeled chair, accompanied by Sister Philips and Molly Turner, the head of the Physiotherapy Department, both of whom had become great friends of hers, were taken by ambulance to Hamilton Terrace. Kathleen was excited and in high spirits, and the men who took her said that never before had they heard so much noise and laughter in an ambulance. The maisonette did not look particularly attractive and the cold dull weather added to its air of dreariness. It had been unoccupied for some months and needed redecorating. After being wheeled into all the rooms downstairs, Kathleen decided that it had possibilities and when she arrived back in

[1] In 1954 it was awarded to her recording of *A Recital of Handel Arias* with the London Philharmonic Orchestra conducted by Sir Adrian Boult, and in 1955 to her recording of Mahler's *Kindertotenlieder* with the Vienna Philharmonic Orchestra conducted by Bruno Walter.

hospital drew a plan of the ground floor and began to think out the best way of arranging the furniture.

Next came the delightful job of looking through wallpaper books and deciding on colour schemes for the various rooms. Soon decorators were busily at work and the time came to pack up everything in the Hampstead flat. Kathleen was most anxious that some of the plants which she had particularly valued, especially the tiny rhododendrons, always referred to as 'my pink pearls', should be transferred to the new garden. This was done.

When the furniture arrived it was put in place according to the plan which Kathleen had drawn. Everything fitted in perfectly. Gradually the house became habitable, but Bernie and Win were in despair about the garden. It was large and neglected and they wondered where to begin.

One evening when they came home a transformation had taken place. Four gardeners were working. The grass was cut, the beds were dug over and plants were being put in. Ruth Draper had arranged a welcome-home present. Not only was the garden put to rights but all the men came every week afterwards to keep it in order.

It was hoped that Kathleen would be able to leave hospital before Easter. She had taken as much treatment as it was possible to give her for the time being and seemed much better. At the end of March 1953 she wrote to the headmistress of her old school:

30th March, 1953.

Dear Miss Gardner,

Thank you so very much for your kind letter. It was lovely to hear from you and your letter has given me great pleasure.

I haven't been to an investiture yet as I have been here for almost seven weeks, but I hope to go to one of the summer investitures. It made a lovely start to the New Year to receive such an award—Win was very excited too, and will go with me to the palace.

I am feeling much better now and leave here on Thursday week —not to Hampstead as there were too many steps to climb—but to a new home at 40 Hamilton Terrace, N.W.8. where there is a lovely garden—to my great joy.

I broke the ligaments and a piece of bone of the hip in the middle of an Orpheus performance, so that is why I have stayed so long here, to give the leg a chance to get strong again. For the time being I must go round in a wheel chair, but I expect I shall soon become expert at steering a middle course and avoid scratching the paint on the doors!

It *was* lovely to hear from you, and I do hope that if by any chance you are in St. John's Wood, you would call, and give me the great pleasure and privilege of welcoming you.

With all good wishes,

Yours affectionately,
Kathleen

(41 on April 22nd!!)

On the Wednesday before Easter Win, on going as usual to hospital after work, found Kathleen ill and depressed. She had had a bilious attack, her temperature had gone up and the nurses thought it unlikely that she would be fit to leave the hospital after all.

Two days later however she was much better again and it was arranged for her to come home the following day. She arrived, accompanied by her two friends, and was delighted with everything. As she sat at the head of the table at lunchtime her face was radiant with happiness.   HOME! HEAVEN! she wrote in her diary.

In the garden was a beautifully upholstered seat, put there on the initiative of Mrs. Franz Osborn, who had collected subscriptions from some of Kathleen's friends in order to provide a 'welcome-home' present. The weather during the next few weeks was good and Kathleen spent much of her time lying on the seat in the sun. Visitors came to see her every day, and she kept a note of their names in her diary. Every evening, after her work at hospital was done, Molly Turner arrived to give her treatment.

Her strength seemed to be increasing and she was able to walk a little in the garden. Having been warned to move carefully and not attempt any steps, she was yet curious about the rooms upstairs. Finding herself alone in the hall one morning, she was overcome with a desire to see them and slowly climbed the stairs. Having had a good look round, she moved cautiously downstairs and returned in triumph to her bed.

For her birthday a party was planned. The food and the wine were provided by Sir John Barbirolli, who also wrote out the menu which consisted of her special favourites, all lovingly prepared by Meme (Sir John's mother) who was always so proud to be asked to do this for the adored Kathleen.

MENU
K.K.

22nd April, 1953.

Prawn Mayonnaise
Southern Fried Chicken
Croquettes of Rice
Cheese — Dessert

————

Bâtard Montrachet   1945
Château Lafite   1945
Melnotte   1943
Cockburn   1912

The Cockburn 1912 was chosen for this occasion to mark 'the forty-first anniversary of the year which had produced a King of Wines and a Queen of Song'. Kathleen wrote in her diary, 'Gorgeous Birthday. Lovely Day.'

Most of her time during the next few weeks was spent in the garden. Jamie and Yvonne Hamilton, who lived opposite, were the source of much pleasure, bringing interesting visitors to see her and overwhelming her with gifts of books and flowers.

Towards the end of April, there took place a dinner party to which Kathleen eagerly looked forward. Princess Margaret had told Hamish Hamilton that she admired Kathleen's voice and would like to meet her again; so the Hamiltons arranged a party, although they were apprehensive as to whether Kathleen's health would permit her to attend. To the last moment Kathleen hoped to sing and her friend Burnet Pavitt was there to accompany her.

Kathleen was brought to the house by Burnet, looking so radiant in full evening dress that no one could have suspected that she was mortally ill. Amazement and delight greeted her arrival, and her fellow guests told her in all sincerity that she had never looked more beautiful. When Princess Margaret appeared, Kathleen stood up, and the Princess said immediately 'Please sit down—I know you have been ill', and herself sat on a stool beside Kathleen's chair to put her at ease. At dinner all went well at first, with Kathleen laughing and talking and apparently enjoying herself. But after an hour she had an attack of nausea and had to leave the table and go home, almost in tears. Princess Margaret was full of solicitude and retained a vivid memory of her courage at that last meeting.

On the 19th May she went to hospital to have X-ray photographs taken. When Win arrived in the evening she found Kathleen in tears. It appeared that after the photographs had been taken they had been propped up against the window, so that she could not help seeing them.

'I didn't want to look at them,' she said, 'but I couldn't help it. They were like a magnet.' The photographs had made her realise how serious her condition was. Win tried to convince her that only a trained person could understand X-ray photographs, but she replied that this had confirmed her conviction that she had been getting steadily worse during the last year. Fortunately Win had brought home some geranium plants for the garden, and when she asked where they were to be planted, Kathleen recovered enough to go out in her wheel chair and direct operations.

The next day she began to suffer from a distressing nausea which continued for several days. It was arranged to take her back into hospital the following Tuesday. The night before she left her beloved new home, Win was startled to see Bernie come in from the garden with tears streaming down her face. 'They're playing Kath's record', she said. In the garden as they stood in the quiet evening air, from the open window of a house came the music of *Das Lied von der Erde,* with Kathleen's voice, full and vibrant singing the *Farewell.*

For a time Kathleen was very ill, and on Coronation Day, 2nd June, she lay between life and death. Gradually, however, her condition improved. A letter from George Baker, the chairman and secretary of the Royal Philharmonic Society awaited the time when she would be well enough to attend to it. It was to offer her the award of the Gold Medal of the Society—one of the most coveted honours in the world of music. No woman singer had received this award since Muriel Foster in 1914. Kathleen dictated her reply and signed it herself.

Although she had gone on hoping to be able to give her recital with Bruno Walter at the Edinburgh Festival, it now became obvious that this would not be possible.

8th June, 1953.

Dearest Kathleen,

I got from Ian Hunter the sad news that you do not believe in the possibility of having the recital with me in Edinburgh. I am sure you will realise the pain which my heart feels, and I want you to know that I think of you daily with the deepest affection and send you all my wishes. Our last common work, the records of Mahler's songs and *Das Lied von der Erde* belong in my mind to the most beautiful musical events of our time, and whoever hears them must respond with an upsurge of admiration and love for you.

Dearest Kathleen, I hope with all my heart to have some better news about you and send you, also from Lotte, our true love.

Yours in friendship.

Bruno Walter.

There was another letter which pleased her:

City Chambers,
Edinburgh, 1.   15th July, 1953.
Dear Miss Ferrier,

I cannot tell you how sorry we all are that you will not be with us at the Festival this summer. Edinburgh at Festival time without Kathleen Ferrier is unbelievable.

I am writing to say how genuinely grieved we all are to learn of your indisposition, and do most sincerely hope that you will make a speedy recovery.

We look forward to future Festivals when you will delight us once again with your singing.

Yours sincerely,
James Miller,
Lord Provost.

About this time her doctors suggested that an American specialist, who was in England for a short time, should be consulted. He discussed her case with the specialist who had seen Kathleen the year before and they advised a further operation. This took place successfully on the 27th July. Kathleen was dangerously ill for a time but then made a wonderful recovery, sitting up in bed, enjoying her meals and talking with her old animation and sparkle.

Soon she said she would like to see some of her 'buddies' again. As she had wanted to see no one but Win, Bernie and Sir John since the previous Whitsun, this was a great step forward. So every evening one or two friends went to visit her, coming out almost weeping with joy to see her so much like her old self again. 'I realise I shall have to be patient', she said. 'The miracle has happened but it will be some time before I regain my strength.'

When the improvement seemed established, Win decided to take a week's holiday, going to the Lake District with a friend. As the days went by, she grew more and more uneasy, and when the telephone rang at lunch time on the Thursday, she knew it was for her and that it was bad news. It was Bernie, asking her to come home. Kathleen had had a relapse.

The last train from Keswick had gone. A hired car just caught the last train from Windermere. By ten o'clock that evening Win was in a taxi on her way to the hospital. Kathleen greeted her with a radiant smile, but there were heavy rings under her eyes and she looked very ill. 'You'll be getting me sacked calling at this time of night', she said, and then, 'I've been proper poorly while you've been away.'

It was hoped that this setback was only temporary, but slowly it became clear that although the operation had removed the pain to a large extent and arrested the disease for a short while, once more it had begun to spread.

Six weeks later Kathleen said to the nurse before she left, 'Wouldn't it be lovely if I could go to sleep and not wake up again.' On the morning of the 8th October she died peacefully.

APPENDIX

Here, taken from her own notebook, is a list of what she sang:

Early English:

The Arch Denial—Arne
*Have you seen but a whyte lily grow—(Elizabethan) *arr.* Grew
*Willow, Willow—(Elizabethan) *arr.* Warlock
Come let's be merry—*arr.* Lane Wilson
Cradle Song—Byrd
Flocks are sporting—Carey
*I will lay me down in peace—Greene
*O Praise the Lord—Greene
Nightingale—Carey
Tell me lovely shepherd—Boyce

Bach:

Prepare Thyself Zion
Bist Du Bei Mir
Ach! dass nicht die letzte Stunde
Vergiss mein nicht
Schlage doch

Brahms:

Mainacht
Der Tod, das ist die kühle Nacht
Immer Leiser wird mein Schlummer
Sonntag
Sapphische Ode
Sonntag Morgen
Wir wandelten
Botschaft
Von ewiger Liebe
Minnelied
Liebestreu
*Vier Ernste Gesänge
*Alto Rhapsody
*Two songs with Viola
Dein blaues Auge
Auf dem See

Brahms (*continued*):

Ruhe Süssliebchen
Heimkehr
Es schauen die Blumen

Beethoven:

Neue Liebe, neues Leben
Ich liebe dich
Tracht night

Chamber Orchestra—own parts:

Star Candles—Michael Head
Hark the ech'ing air—Purcell
Where'er you walk—Handel
Dearest Consort—Handel
Art thou troubled—Handel
Cradle Song—Byrd
Che faro senza Euridice—Gluck
Water Boy—*arr.* Robinson
My Boy Willie—*arr.* Sharp
I have a bonnet—*arr.* Hughes
Four poems of St. Theresa—Lennox Berkeley

Cornelius:

Brautliebe

British Songs:

Spring—Ivor Gurney
Down by the Salley Gardens—Ivor Gurney
*Sleep—Peter Warlock
*Pretty Ring Time—Peter Warlock
Three Psalms—Rubbra
*Silent Noon—Vaughan Williams
Song of the Pilgrims—Vaughan Williams
Star Candles—Michael Head
Sweet chance—Michael Head
The Piper—Michael Head
Little Road to Bethlehem—Michael Head
October Valley—Michael Head
*Love is a Bable—Parry
*Go not happy day—Frank Bridge

British Songs (continued):

    *The Fairy Lough—Stanford
    *A Soft Day—Stanford
    Bold Unbiddable Child—Stanford
    La Belle dame Sans Merci—Stanford
    By a Bier side—Armstrong Gibbs
    Sigh no more—Aikin
    Rahoon—Moeran
    Merry Greenwood—Moeran
    To Daisies—Quilter
    *Over the mountains—Quilter
    *Now sleeps the crimson petal—Quilter
    *Fair house of joy—Quilter
    *Drink to me only—Quilter
    *Ye banks and braes—Quilter
    The White Peace—Bax
    Lullaby—Cyril Scott
    The Heart worships—Holst
    Twilight Fancies—Delius
    Close thine eyes—Mary Plumstead

Folk Songs:

    *My bonny Lad—Traditional
    I will give my love an apple—Traditional
    O men from the fields—*arr.* Hughes
    *O Waly, Waly—*arr.* Britten
    *Come you not from Newcastle?—*arr.* Britten
    *I know where I'm going—*arr.* Hughes, *adapt.* Gray
    She walked thro' the fair—*arr.* Hughes
    *I have a bonnet—*arr.* Hughes
    The Spanish Lady—*arr.* Hughes
    *Kitty my love will you marry me—*arr.* Hughes
    *My Boy Willie—*arr.* Sharp
    Swing Low—*arr.* Robinson
    Water Boy—*arr.* Robinson
    *Fidgety Bairn—*arr.* Roberton
    *Ca' the Yowes—*arr.* Jacobson
    Shenandoah—*arr.* Jacobson
    Ash Grove—*arr.* Britten
    Oliver Cromwell—*arr.* Britten
    O can ye sew cushions—*arr.* Roberton
    *Down by the Salley Gardens—Gurney
    *I will walk with my love—*arr.* Hughes
    B for Barney—*arr.* Hughes

Folk Songs (continued):

    *The Lovers Curse—*arr.* Hughes
    *Blow the wind southerly—*arr.* Whittaker
    *Keel Row—*arr.* Whittaker
    Bobby Shaftoe—*arr.* Whittaker
    *Stuttering Lovers—*arr.* Hughes

Fauré:

    Nell
    Lydia
    Au bord de l'eau
    Après un rêve

Giordano:

    Caro mio ben

Gluck:

    Orfeo

Handel:

    *Art thou troubled
    Pack Clouds Away
    How changed the vision
    Dearest Consort
    Verdant Meadows
    *Spring
    *Come to me soothing sleep
    Where'er you walk
    Lascio chio pianga
    Sweet Rose and Lily
    *Ombra mai fu
    Like as the love lorn turtle

Italian Songs:

    Pur dicesti—Lotti
    Lasciatemi morire—Monteverdi
    Che faro—Gluck

Mahler:

  Wo die schönen Trompeten blasen
  Ich ging mit Lust
  *Ich bin der Welt
  *Ich atmet einen Linden duft
  *Um Mitternacht

Kabalevsky:

  Old King Cole
  I saw a ship a-sailing
  If all the seas were one sea

With Orchestra:

  *Kindertotenlieder—Mahler
  *Das Lied von der Erde—Mahler
  Ombra felice—Mozart
  *Four Serious Songs—Brahms
  *Alto Rhapsody—Brahms
  Poème de l'Amour et de la Mer—Chausson
  Schlage doch, gewünschte Stunde—Bach
  Prepare thyself Zion—Bach
  Ebarme dich—Bach
  Spring Symphony—Britten
  Who is Sylvia?—Schubert
  The Enchantress—Bliss
  Sea Pictures—Elgar

Operatic:

  *Che Faro—Gluck
  Adieu forêts—Tschaikowsky

Purcell:

  Mad Bess—*arr.* Britten
  There's not a Swain—*arr.* Britten
  Hark the ech'ing air
  Evening Hymn
  Fairest Isle
  When I am laid in earth
  I attempt from love's sickness to fly

Schumann:

  *Frauenliebe und Leben

Schumann (*continued*):

  *Widmung
  Volkslieder
  Ich grolle nicht

Schubert:

  *An die Musik
  Suleika I & II
  Rosamunde
  *Die junge Nonne
  *Grechen am Spinnrade
  Haiden-röslein
  Du liebst mich nicht
  *Der Musensohn
  Erster Verlust
  Erlkönig
  Rastlose Liebe
  Nur wer die Sehnsucht kennt
  Wanderers Nachtlied
  Who is Sylvia?
  Hark, hark the Lark
  Lachen und Weinen
  Tod und das Mädchen
  Der Jüngling an der Quelle
  An die Leyer
  Ganymed

Strauss:

  Morgen

Wolf:

  Verborgenheit
  Gärtner
  Auf ein altes Bild
  Auf einer Wanderung
  Weyla's Gesang

Oratorio :

Bach:

  *Cantatas No. 11, 67
  *St. Matthew Passion—Grief for Sin

Bach (*continued*):

*St. John Passion—All is Fulfilled
*Mass in B Minor—Qui sedes
*   Agnus Dei
Christmas Oratorio
Magnificat

Elgar:

Dream of Gerontius
The Apostles
The Kingdom

Handel:

*Messiah—O Thou that Tellest. He Was Despised
*Samson—Return O God of Hosts
*Judas Maccabaeus—Father of Heaven
*Israel in Egypt

Mendelssohn:

*Elijah—O Rest in the Lord. Woe Unto Them

Pergolesi:

*Stabat Mater

Carols:

*Silent Night, Holy Night—*arr*. Fagan
*O Come All Ye Faithful—*arr*. Fagan

* Recorded.

BLOW THE WIND SOUTHERLY

[*Traditional*

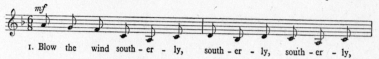

1. Blow the wind south - er - ly, south - er - ly, south - er - ly,

Blow the wind south o'er the bon - ny blue sea;

Blow the wind south - er - ly, south - er - ly, south - er - ly,

Blow bon - ny breeze, my lov - er to me. _____ They

told me last night there were ships in the off - ing, And

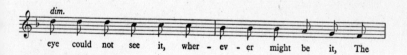

I hur - ried down to the deep roll - ing sea; But my

eye could not see it, wher - ev - er might be it, The

bark that is bear - ing my lov - er to me.

UM MITTERNACHT

Um Mit - ter - nacht hab' - ich ge -wacht und auf -ge blickt zum Him-mel! Kein Stern vom Stern ge wim - mel hat mir ge - lacht um Mit - ter - nacht!

How pure the light! How clear the sun! Such shin — —ing brightness ne'er have I seen! How sweet these sounds I hear a - bout me.

Translation used at Covent Garden, Feb. 1953